Mind your (English) Language with CGP!

Doing well in GCSE English Language involves a lot more than just speaking the lingo. You'll need to really get stuck in to the fine details of reading and writing...

Not to worry. This brilliant CGP Workbook is packed with essential practice — from exercises that test you on the basics to realistic exam-style questions. And of course, it's all perfectly matched to the new WJEC Eduqas course.

We've also included worked exam papers with sample answers for you to mark, a full set of practice papers and all the answers! If we'd thought the kitchen sink would help you get a top grade, we'd have included that too.

CGP — still the best! ☺

Our sole aim here at CGP is to produce the highest quality books — carefully written, immaculately presented and dangerously close to being funny.

Then we work our socks off to get them out to you — at the cheapest possible prices.

CONTENTS

CONTENTS

Published by CGP

Editors:
Joe Brazier
Emma Crighton

With thanks to Glenn Rogers and Nicola Woodfin for the proofreading.
With thanks to Ana Pungartnik for the copyright research.

Acknowledgements:

With thanks to iStock.com for permission to use the images on pages 2, 17, 18, 32 & 60.

_Letter written by Charlotte Brontë on page 78 from 'Charlotte Brontë and Her Circle',
by Clement K. Shorter, 1896 (pages 80-82)._

Article entitled 'Confessions of a Nanny' on page 79 © Guardian News & Media Ltd 2016.

_Extract from 'The Night' by Ray Bradbury on pages 91-92 reprinted by permission of Abner Stein © 1946
by Weird Tales, renewed 1973 by Ray Bradbury._

Article entitled 'What are friends for?' on page 95 © Guardian News & Media Ltd 2016.

_Every effort has been made to locate copyright holders and obtain permission to reproduce sources.
For those sources where it has been difficult to trace the copyright holder of the work, we would be grateful
for information. If any copyright holder would like us to make an amendment to the acknowledgements,
please notify us and we will gladly update the book at the next reprint. Thank you._

ISBN: 978 1 78294 372 3
Printed by Elanders Ltd, Newcastle upon Tyne.
Clipart from Corel®

Based on the classic CGP style created by Richard Parsons.

Planning Answers

Q1 Read this exam question, then answer the questions below.

> **Read lines 12-21 of the source.**
> How does the writer describe Uncle William?

a) Underline the phrase which tells you what part of the text to write about.

b) Which character should your answer focus on? ....

Q2 Here's an exam question and a plan for an answer. Write down **three** reasons why it's a good plan.

> You have read a report which says that it is important for young people to participate in sport.
>
> **Write a lively newspaper article in which you explain your point of view on what the report has said.**
>
> <u>Plan</u>
>
> Positive view on report: benefits of sport e.g. learning teamwork.
> My counter-argument 1: young people are busy; may not have time.
> My counter-argument 2: can get the benefits of sport in other ways.
> Conclusion: Sport is good, but we don't all have to do it.

The lack of young people involved in sport was becoming problematic for the Olympic team.

1) ....

2) ....

3) ....

Q3 Write a brief plan for an answer to the question below.

> Your school wants to give all students aged 11-16 a pet to care for.
>
> You have decided to write a speech to be given to your school governors to share your views on this idea. You could write in favour or against this idea.
>
> **Write an engaging speech giving your views.**

....

....

....

....

Don't just stare into space — get on and planet...

You don't need to plan every answer in your English Language exams, but for the longer writing questions (Section B in each paper) it's important. Tick the self-assessment boxes below to show how well you think you've done on this page.

 ☐   ☐   ☐

P.E.E.D.

Q1 Read the following exam answers. Tick the answers which use the P.E.E.D. technique (Point, Example, Explain, Develop).

a) The writer uses similes to make his description of Kidston's motor racing more vivid. For example, he describes Kidston's Bentley as being "like a cheetah". This shows how powerful and fast Kidston's car was. This phrase also connects Kidston with a cheetah, suggesting that he is exciting and exotic too.

b) The writer says that the racing driver Glen Kidston was rich, glamorous and charismatic. He had an exciting career in the Royal Navy, surviving several torpedo attacks, before taking up motor sports. He won the Le Mans 24-hour race in 1930, but died in a plane crash in the Drakensberg Mountains in 1931, aged just 32.

c) The writer uses rhetorical questions to get the reader to agree with their point of view. For example, he asks "Was there a finer, more determined driver than Kidston?" The rhetorical questions lead the reader to agree with the writer's opinion that Kidston was a great driver, and make the whole text more persuasive.

☐   ☐   ☐

Q2 Read the following extract from a tourist information sheet.

West Kennet Long Barrow — The Skeleton Tomb

West Kennet Long Barrow is an ancient tomb near Avebury. Here you can become a real-life tomb explorer, and experience the thrill of having history at your fingertips. There are five fascinating chambers in the tomb, where you can explore, quest and hunt to discover the secrets of a bygone age. This is probably the best-preserved tomb of its kind in the country — a real archeological treat for all ages.

© iStock.com/Nastco

Write out an example from the text that you could use to support each point below. Then explain why your example supports the point.

a) Point: *The writer uses direct address to form a personal link with the reader.*

Example: ....

Explanation: ....

....

b) Point: *The writer also uses a combination of descriptive verbs to create a sense of adventure.*

Example: ....

Explanation: ....

....

P.E.E.D.

Q3   Read the following extract from the opening to a short story, and answer the questions below.

> Alice stepped from the bus and was immediately hit by a rush of smells and noises that filled her with the thrill of the new and unknown. She blinked at the bright tropical sun and strode forward into the enticing hustle and bustle of Bangkok.
>
> She didn't really know where her feet were taking her, but she knew that there were a thousand things she wanted to do. Where to begin? The Grand Palace? The market? A stroll along the river? It all had to be done, but the order was open to debate.
>
> Alice reached in her satchel for her guide book, but she hesitated as her fingers brushed its pages. No, she wasn't going to do this like other people had done it; she was going to do it her way and it'd be all the better for it. Stashing the guide book, she decided that the first adventure would be to follow her eager nose to the market stalls.

a)   How is Alice feeling in this extract?

....

b)   Write out an example from the text that supports your answer.

....

....

c)   Explain how your example shows how Alice is feeling.

....

....

....

d)   Now develop your point.

....

....

....

CGP Useless Fact #1872 — a joke can always be made about P.E.E.D. ...

If there's a secret to doing well in English exams, it's probably this: the P.E.E.D. framework is an absolutely brilliant way of writing top-notch answers. It ensures that all of your points are backed up, explained and fully developed. Nifty, eh?

4

Writing Well

Q1 Exam answers should be written in Standard English. For each pair of sentences below, underline the sentence that is written in Standard English.

a) When all's said and done, the writer in Source A is way more positive about breeding cats.

Overall, the writer in Source A demonstrates a more positive attitude towards breeding cats.

b) The writer in Source B doesn't include other people's point of view, so they're very biased.

The writer in Source B doesn't, like, consider other people's views, so they're really biased.

c) The writer in Source B tries to get you on side with their own sob story about cat breeding.

The writer in Source B tries to convince the reader using an anecdote about cat breeding.

Q2 Rewrite each sentence below so that it is in Standard English.

a) The metaphor "a furious battleground" suggests that the house is proper chaotic and stuff.

....

....

b) When Sam and Nina are talking it tells you how them characters are feeling.

....

....

Q3 Fill in the blanks in the passage below using the explaining words and phrases in the box.

signifying   furthermore   emphasises   reinforce

The writer uses short sentences, which increase the pace of the text and build tension. They also help to .... the sense of urgency, and so help the reader to imagine Sadie's panic. ...., the setting adds to the suspense. The writer .... the stormy conditions that Sadie is trapped in, ... that she's vulnerable.

Writing Well

Q4 Circle the **four** words and phrases which you could use to link paragraphs in an exam answer.

Another point of view is	Secondly	metaphor	Highlights
Conversely	Safe to say	Don't get me wrong	In addition to this

Q5 Rewrite the following answer. Break it down into **three** paragraphs and add appropriate words or phrases to make the paragraphs link smoothly together.

> The extract from the biography argues that Orson Welles' career was a "magnificent failure". It points to the fact that his greatest achievement, 'Citizen Kane', was made before the age of thirty. The magazine article argues that Orson Welles was a wonderful director and actor throughout his career. It suggests that people like the "myth" of Orson Welles' fall from grace and ignore his later achievements. The third text, the interview with Orson Welles, shows that he himself had conflicting feelings towards his career and achievements. The interviewer describes him as "fiercely proud" of his films, but also "insecure beneath the bravado".

....

....

....

....

....

....

....

....

....

....

....

....

....

Writing... writing... writing — **this writing well has an echo...**

Obscure 'well' jokes aside, these pages are full of useful tips for your exam answers. Here's a recap: use Standard English, include a good variety of explaining and linking words or phrases and, whatever you do, don't forget to use paragraphs.

Reading with Insight

Q1 Draw lines to match each passage below with the writer's intended meaning.

a) The sky was a vivacious blue, uninterrupted by cloud
— Claire could imagine exactly how the cool lake
would look beneath it. She crossed another date off
her calendar with a gratifying flick of red marker pen.

The character is feeling exhausted.

b) At last, after an hour spent coaxing the stubborn lever,
Peter's seat reclined. He slowly lowered himself
backwards, finally allowing his drooping eyelids to close.
The sounds of the motorway seemed to instantly lull.

The character is looking forward to something.

c) Suddenly, dishes of every type of cuisine flew in from doors
around the hall, assaulting Tomek's senses and ensnaring
him in a haze of sticky and somewhat nauseating scents.
He reached for his glass of water with a sweaty hand.

The character is feeling uncomfortable.

Q2 Read the following text and then complete the table below.

The films Alfred Hitchcock made in the 1950s and 1960s contain tantalising
glimpses of greatness. Iconic images from these films stick in the mind, for example
Janet Leigh screaming in the shower in 'Psycho'.

However, when looking at Hitchcock's career as a whole, it is his earlier films from
the 1930s and 1940s which still delight. Early features like 'The 39 Steps' and 'The Lady
Vanishes' have a wonderful humour and lightness of touch. In contrast, his later films,
even classics like 'Vertigo' and 'The Birds', are often leaden in their pace and tone.

One reason for the change in quality of Hitchcock's films was the way he gorged
himself on the worship he received as he got older. Younger film directors like François
Truffaut revered him. This swelled Hitchcock's already substantial ego, and contributed
to an increasingly dull, self-conscious style of film.

Pretentious film students might still extol the virtues of the 'classics', but I'd rather
watch one of those early, off-the-cuff, Hitchcock masterpieces any day.

Words and phrases which imply the writer dislikes Hitchcock's later films	Words and phrases which imply the writer likes Hitchcock's early films	Words and phrases which imply the writer dislikes Hitchcock as a person
1.	1.	1.
2.	2.	2.

Reading with Insight

Q3 Pick out **one** word or phrase from the text which shows you that the writer wants the restaurant owner to feel apologetic. Then explain why it tells you this.

> I was sorely disappointed last weekend when the standard of food fell well below what I had come to expect from your restaurant. As a loyal and regular customer, I hope you will be forthcoming in providing either reimbursement or a voucher, since I felt cheated in having to pay on this occasion.

Claire wasn't sure what her meal was supposed to be, but she was fairly sure it wasn't the burger she'd ordered.

Example: ....

Explanation: ....

....

....

Q4 Read the following extract:

> Ed shifted his weight from one foot to another and stared through the Saturday crowds, trying to see her among them. She said she'd be here at noon. He checked his phone for the umpteenth time: no messages. He glanced back through the crowds, and of course, there she was, walking right towards him. His stomach churned and he felt his heart beat just a little harder. She caught sight of him, smiled and waved. He couldn't help but grin right back at her. He dug his hand into his pocket and his fingers found the small, velvet box. He was going to do it: he was going to ask her, today at the restaurant. He took a deep breath as she came closer. He didn't want to give himself away.
>
> "Are you alright?" she asked, having given him a peck on the cheek. "You look a bit peaky."
> "I'm fine," he lied, taking her by the hand. "Happy to see you, of course."

Explain how Ed is feeling in this passage. Give evidence from the text to support your answer.

....

....

....

....

....

I tried to read with insight — I went cross-eyed...

When you read a text, you'll often feel like you just 'know' what the writer's intention is — that's because they've been very clever and made you feel a certain way. The trick is to look more closely at the text to see how they've done that.

8

Spelling, Punctuation and Grammar

Q1 Put commas and full stops where they're needed into the sentences below.

    a) I jumped out of the taxi narrowly missing a very large puddle by the kerb

    b) Keeley said she wanted a tablet a pair of shoes and some more make-up

    c) As the boat glided past its bright paint glinting in the sun I was able
       to see the captain saluting me his gold braid fluttering in the breeze

Q2 Tick the boxes next to the words that are spelt correctly. Correct the words spelt incorrectly by putting brackets around each word, crossing it out neatly, and then writing the correction above.

arguement	☐	unnatural	☐	concsious	☐	figarative	☐
neccessarily	☐	disappear	☐	immediately	☐	consience	☐
favorite	☐	embarassed	☐	decieved	☐	occasional	☐

Q3 Copy the sentences below, replacing the full stops and commas with semicolons, question marks or exclamation marks where appropriate.

As far as time-travel destinations went, the Ice Age had been a poor choice.

    a) I didn't want to go. The leaden sky threatened rain.

    ....

    ....

    b) Have you ever wondered what it would be like to travel in time. It'd be fantastic.

    ....

    ....

    c) You can come to my party as long as you bring an expensive present, lovingly wrapped, stay until the end, which will be 2 am, clear up any spillages, and serve the drinks.

    ....

    ....

    ....

Spelling, Punctuation and Grammar

Q4 Rewrite the sentences below, correcting the grammatical errors in each one.

a) There wasn't no reason to had a fire drill during the exam.

....

b) Hannah should of eaten the sandwich before it's expiry date.

....

Q5 Rewrite the passage below, correcting the **eight** spelling, punctuation and grammar mistakes.

> As he stepped out of the exam hall on that tuesday morning, Rashid breathed an enormous sigh of relief. He wouldn't need to do no more practice papers, and his days of revision and stress were finished. He could of shouted with joy. It was over, and hopefully it had been worth it. He felt the scientific equations evaporates from his mind like morning dew. As Rashid leant gently against the wall to steady himself, he was overcome by the nowledge that his life was now his. He weren't sure exactly what it would bring, but that was part of the excitement

....

....

....

....

....

....

....

....

....

....

I brought a wand to my first spelling lesson — it was all a bit of a let-down...

It was also the day my hopes of becoming a wizard were cruelly dashed... Oh, the harsh lessons of life. Sadly, here's another harsh lesson — poor spelling, punctuation and grammar will cost you marks. Make sure you know your stuff.

Finding Information and Ideas

Q1 Read the text below.

> Dani approached the roller coaster with wide eyes. She had never been a big fan of rides, but her friend Mel had offered to give £20 to charity if Dani agreed to ride the biggest roller coaster in the park — a towering steel beast with four loops and six corkscrew turns. Her stomach churned at the thought.
> "You can do it, Dani," Mel said, squeezing her shoulder. "You might even enjoy it!"

Dani kept insisting she wasn't a big fan, but the rotating blades and constant whirring suggested otherwise.

Tick the **one** statement that is true.

a) Dani's friend Mel loves theme park rides. ☐

b) Dani is nervous about going on the roller coaster. ☐

c) It was Dani's idea to get sponsored to go on the ride. ☐

Q2 Underline the words and phrases which show that the writer has a negative view of the zoo.

> Last weekend we found ourselves with nothing to do on a warm, sunny day, so we decided on a trip to the zoo. The entrance to the zoo was via a rusty iron gate that looked in serious need of repair. We went into the ticket office, only to discover that the floor was filthy; as we looked closer, we realised there was revolting leftover food scattered everywhere. Inside, the animals looked malnourished and miserable in their enclosures, which all seemed dull and empty, with precious little space for them to run around. All in all, a pretty depressing place.

Q3 From lines 3-8 of the text below, write down **three** facts about the garden.

> 1 "If the boiler hadn't broken, we'd have enough money to go to Hawaii by now," said
> 2 Tim glumly, skirting a puddle of mud in order to peg the laundry onto the washing line.
> 3 Alex frowned and sat down heavily on the bench, which took up almost all of the
> 4 space in their tiny back garden.
> 5 "I bet it's sunny there," she said wistfully, pulling her cardigan in closer.
> 6 The wind was whistling a discordant chorus through the gaps in the fence, making
> 7 the damp grass shiver. The gnarled, stunted apple tree in the corner emitted an
> 8 ominously loud groan that made Tim jump.

1) ....

2) ....

3) ....

Finding Information and Ideas

Now you've got the theory sorted, it's time to put it into practice with these exam-style questions.

Q4   Read the following extract from a novel.

> The doorbell rang. Someone must have answered it, because moments later I heard George's nasal tones in the hallway.
> "So lovely to be here!" he cried, his voice carrying easily across the living room.
> "Did you invite him?" I hissed, staring desperately at Rosa.
> "I could hardly leave him out," she said coolly. "It would have been too obvious."
> He entered the room. His garish purple suit and elaborate hairstyle made him stand out sharply from the other guests. "George, darling," Rosa cooed. "You made it."
> "Rosa!" he said, presenting her with a bottle of cheap-looking wine. "And Freddie," he said to me with a smirk, extending a greasy hand adorned with several gaudy rings. "Good to see you."
> "You too," I said, forcing a smile and letting go of his hand quickly. "Drink?"
> "Oh, go on then," said George, "I'd love a nice whisky, if you have any?"
> "Nothing but the best for you, George," I replied through gritted teeth.

List **five** facts from the text about George.

Q5   Read the following extract from a review of a holiday park, then answer the questions underneath.

> You would need a fortnight to try all the activities at Lowbridge Park. From abseiling to zorbing, the park offers a mind-boggling range of activities. I was only there for a long weekend, so I had to prioritise!
> I began with a pony trek. Although it drizzled the entire morning, it was a great way to explore the woodland. In the afternoon I debated between rock climbing and mountain biking. I settled on the former, primarily to stay out of the rain!
> The next day, the weather was better, so my choice fell between canoeing and sailing. I settled for a canoe and headed out on the lake, which was stunning early in the morning. The good weather lasted into the afternoon, which meant that I was also lucky enough to be able to go paragliding. What an exhilarating experience!
> I decided to finish my trip with a spot of archery. Alas, I'm no Robin Hood, but the instructor was patient, and I improved a little over the course of the morning.

a) How long does the writer think it would take to try everything at Lowbridge Park?   ....

b) Why did the writer decide to go rock climbing?   ....

c) What was the writer's final activity at the park?   ....

List five reasons why you love studying for GCSE English — umm...

Some questions will simply ask you to find information and ideas in a text. That doesn't sound like too tough a task, but remember that sometimes you'll need to read between the lines a bit — it won't always be dead obvious, I'm afraid.

Summarising Information and Ideas

Q1   Summarise the two views given in the text below.

> Human beings have eaten meat for millions of years. Meat-eaters argue that we have evolved with the ability to eat and digest meat, proving that it forms a natural part of the human diet. Furthermore, meat contains many vitamins and minerals, particularly iron, that are important for human function.
>
> However, vegetarians argue that, biologically, we have very little in common with other species of meat-eaters. For example, we lack the ability to kill an animal and take its meat without tools. Additionally, they argue that a high consumption of red meat contributes to a range of health problems in humans, such as cardiovascular disease and some cancers.

Meat-eaters: ....

....

Vegetarians: ....

....

Q2   Using information from **both** texts below, give **one** reason why people should learn to play a musical instrument. Give **one** piece of evidence from each text to support your answer.

19th-Century Letter
My beloved son,
    It is my dearest wish that you devote yourself to your music lessons once more. The happiness it will bring me can only be equalled by the happiness such a pastime will incite in your own soul. Furthermore, you will also learn the skill of perseverance, which will surely have a positive effect on the rest of your studies.

21st-Century Report
Several reliable studies have shown that students aged 11-16 who play an instrument achieve a greater proportion of passing grades in their GCSE exams; furthermore, there is anecdotal evidence to suggest that these students average higher levels of general happiness than their peers.

Reason: ....

Evidence from 19th-century text: ....

....

Evidence from 21st-century text: ....

....

Summarising Information and Ideas

Q3 Read the following extracts.

19th-Century Letter

Dearest Jane,

I have just come to the end of a most fascinating novel. Increasingly, I find myself considering reading to be the most entertaining way to occupy oneself. I tire easily of needlework, and music bores me, but I could, and do, read on for hours and hours. I have learnt about many fascinating places that I could never hope to visit myself, all from my own little chair, or whilst travelling in my carriage.

21st-Century Newspaper Article

Despite the waning popularity of reading amongst the younger generation, I think there's still something to be said for losing yourself in a good book. What other hobby can you do for hours on end without getting bored?

Long train journeys, beach holidays, cosy Sunday afternoons — it doesn't matter where you are, reading is always a convenient and enjoyable activity.

What's more, reading widens your horizons — I've learnt more from books than I ever did from my school teachers.

According to these two writers, why should people read books?

Q4 Read the following extracts.

19th-Century Diary

Today we had the pleasure of visiting the DeWhitt family at Huntingham Castle. With its riverside situation and fine grounds and gardens, the castle was perfectly outfitted to provide an enjoyable day's entertainment for our two families.

Perhaps the most agreeable aspect of the visit was the turn we took around the art galleries, where portraits of the DeWhitt family line the walls in a parade of solemn splendour — a thoroughly impressive collection.

21st-Century Review

Huntingham Castle really does have something for everybody. Art fan? Check out the incredible portrait gallery. Into scenic views? The gardens are divine, and there's a picturesque river flowing through the far reaches of the castle grounds. In short, you really can't fail to love the place! As an added bonus, there's a train station situated close by, so even getting there is an absolute breeze.

According to these two writers, why should people visit Huntingham Castle?

In summary — learn how to summarise information and ideas...

Summarising texts is an important skill that you'll need to master — in paper 2 you'll be asked to write a summary about a particular topic. Practice makes perfect — the more you practise writing concise summaries, the easier it will get.

Audience and Purpose

Q1   For each sentence, circle the word which best describes its intended audience.

     a) "Do you yearn for a simpler, more reliable way of managing your finances?"   **children / adults**

     b) "When buying a used car, try to get as much information from the dealer as you can."   **experts / novices**

When buying a used toilet roll — don't.

Q2   Draw lines to match each text to its main purpose.

     a) "Shop around for the best quote — some insurers are much more expensive than others."   **To entertain**

     b) "As the train moved south, first crawling, then increasing to a steady gallop, the scenery gradually changed from the flat and drab to the dramatic and beautiful."   **To persuade**

     c) "Who could disagree with the fact that children should eat healthily?"   **To advise**

Q3   Find **two** words or phrases that show this text is aimed at a younger audience, and explain how they show this.

Are you looking for a cool summer job?

We've got loads of temporary vacancies with no experience required!

All you need is some free time over the holidays, a positive attitude and plenty of energy. If you've got your own wheels that's even better!

With Spondon Summer Jobs you can:
- gain real-world work experience
- earn a few quid
- make new friends

Whatever you fancy, we can find you a job that suits you down to the ground! Interested? Call Jackie on 0547 262 626 or find us on social media.

Word or phrase: ....

Explanation: ....

....

Word or phrase: ....

Explanation: ....

....

Audience and Purpose

Try these exam-style questions, then use the self-assessment boxes to mark how well you think you did.

 Q4 Read the following extract from a leaflet advertising an aquarium.

> **Come to Oxton Aquarium — you'll have a whale of a time!**
>
> At Oxton Aquarium you can see lots of different sea creatures all in one place. You could be eyed up by an octopus, shaken by a shark or peered at by a pike! They're all here in our very special underwater world — and we're open every day in the school holidays.
>
> Whether you come with your school, your family or your friends, you're bound to have a fantastic time.
>
> "I've had the best day ever. Can we go round again?" — Adam Rodgers, age 9.
>
> Oxton Aquarium is a fun and fishy day out that you'll never forget!

How has the writer adapted their language to engage their audience?

 Q5 Read the following extract from a newspaper opinion piece.

> Is it really that time of year again? The decorations go up and suddenly the nation is whipped up into a frenzy, convinced that the only way to survive the coming holiday is to grab a trolley and raid the supermarket. We stock up as if an apocalypse is coming, buying up vast quantities of everything from over-priced tins of chocolate right down to the last bruised parsnip.
>
> It's time we admitted that the whole process is utterly ridiculous. Don't get me wrong, I love Christmas. I love the decorations, the merriment and, most of all, the abundance of delicious food. But what simply must end is the bizarre mentality that causes us to frantically race to the shops five minutes before closing time on Christmas Eve. We've all been there, haven't we? Running around like headless chickens, gripped by a sudden and deathly terror that we might not have stockpiled enough after-dinner mints to last the festivities.
>
> Britain, we need to take a stand against festive stress. Christmas is a special time of year; it should be a time to sit back and take a break from the stresses of everyday life. So please, enjoy your holiday — and try to remember that the world won't end should you happen to forget the cranberry sauce.

The writer is trying to persuade the audience to agree with their views about Christmas. How do they try to do this?

I took a stand once — I needed something to put my sheet music on...

As it turns out, it's surprisingly difficult to make a living playing the nose flute, but that's beside the point. Audience and purpose are really important in your exam, so use the questions on these pages to really nail your understanding of them.

16

Informative and Entertaining Texts

Q1   Put an **I** next to the statements that are informative, and an **E** next to the entertaining ones.

a) "Steven Morrissey was born in Manchester on 22nd May 1959."

☐

b) "The gig was absolute mayhem. Swathes of bodies ebbed and flowed in a sea of delirium — enjoyment and a survival instinct competed for my attention."

☐

c) "The next event at Spark Bridge village hall is a performance by Jim Dodd and the Budgies, at 7.30 pm on December 12th."

☐

Q2   Underline **two** words or phrases in the text below which suggest that its purpose is to entertain. Then explain why these examples suggest this on the lines below.

> The woman was incredibly old. Her back was bent permanently by the sheer weight of the years she'd lived, and her skin was papery thin, revealing a labyrinth of thick blue veins that crisscrossed her trembling hands.
> She spoke quietly and kindly to the lost child, then, once he had stopped crying, gently guided him to sit down on a nearby bench. As they walked, the discordant clink and clank of her jewellery sang through the air.

....

....

....

Q3   Read the text below, which is from the travel section of a newspaper.

> Public bathing may not be a familiar experience to a British tourist, but the tranquillity of the beautiful Gellért Baths are enough to convert even the most apprehensive of travellers. Here, bathers luxuriate across eight thermal pools, each of a different temperature. The hottest pool (an immersive 40 degrees) soothed my sightseeing-weary muscles as well as any massage I've ever received.

a) Write down **two** facts about the Gellért Baths that you can learn from this text.

Fact 1: ....

Fact 2: ....

b) Explain how the writer has presented **one** of these facts in an engaging way.

....

....

Section Two — Reading: Understanding Texts

Informative and Entertaining Texts

It's time for some more exam-style questions. Remember to use the self-assessment boxes when you're done.

 Q4 Read the following extract from a short story.

> For her thirteenth birthday, Jasmine's parents had bought her a hockey stick. The thought process behind this baffling decision was a total mystery. They should have known better than anyone that she wasn't remotely interested in sport. Wasn't it obvious? She was nearing the point of needing to be surgically removed from her game console, and she had already mastered the art of the forged sick note. Lounging on the sofa was her passion — one to which she dedicated herself with all the staunch tenacity of an Olympic athlete. Going outside with her parents, meanwhile, was more daunting than an icy trek over an Arctic precipice. She wasn't at all hopeful for a sudden transformation of her sofa-bound self into a hockey-stick wielding, goal-scoring demon. Those girls terrified her. She was Jasmine the gamer, a silent lone wolf. She was not, nor would she ever be, Jasmine the whooping and cheering team-player.

"The writer is successful in entertaining the reader. She brings the different sides of Jasmine's personality to light." To what extent do you agree with this statement?

 Q5 Read the following text from a history magazine.

The Battle of Hastings was fought on October 14th 1066, on a field near Hastings in East Sussex. Led by William the Conqueror, it was the Normans' most important victory over the Anglo-Saxons.

William's army was a well-trained body of respected fighters. In contrast to Harold's army, which consisted mostly of foot soldiers, William's force had significant numbers of cavalry and archers — the cavalry sat proudly atop horses bred specially for their strength. At the helm of the Norman host stood a man with years of military experience.

Beginning at around nine o'clock in the morning, the battle was furious and bloody, and vast numbers of soldiers were brutally slain. At one stage, the English, led by King Harold II, were fooled into thinking they had won the battle, so they stormed towards their enemy, only to be mercilessly ambushed and trampled like insects.

© iStock.com/Butsaya

The writer is trying to both inform and entertain the reader. How do they try to do this?

Entertaining texts — I thought mobile phones weren't allowed in the exam...
Entertaining and informing are at opposite ends of the spectrum in lots of ways, but they can also be combined. Keep an eye out for texts with multiple purposes in the exam — spotting them is often the ticket to a good answer.

     Section Two — Reading: Understanding Texts

Texts that Argue, Persuade or Advise

Q1   Draw lines to match each statement below to its purpose.

a) "The barbaric practice of bear-baiting must be stopped completely and immediately."

To argue

b) "If you want to make a difference, there are many organisations you can sign up to."

To persuade

c) "By joining our march and signing this petition, you will be helping to put an end to this disgraceful act of cruelty."

To advise

Q2   Read the following text.

> Flamingos are the most fascinating birds in the world. Their beguiling beauty is unrivalled in the animal kingdom. Should such beauty go unsupported?
> I'm starting a vital campaign to sponsor flamingos in zoos. By donating just a few pounds, you can help fund the establishment of breeding programmes for these most special of birds. The head keeper at my local zoo, Jane Sutton, says, "Flamingos really are wonderful animals. A dedicated breeding programme would be invaluable to their endurance as a species."

© iStock.com/Anna Omelchenko

The table below shows the techniques used by the writer to persuade the reader. Fill in the table by picking out examples of each technique.

Technique	Example from text
rhetorical question	
opinion stated as fact	
expert opinion	
direct address to the reader	

Q3   Choose **one** word or phrase from the text below which shows that its purpose is to advise. Then explain how it helps the writer to achieve this purpose.

> It's easy to get bogged down in all the choices when you're choosing a new mobile phone, but don't worry — there are plenty of people out there to help you. You could consider going into a phone shop to chat to an expert, or check out a handy online forum.

Example: ....

Explanation: ....

....

Texts that Argue, Persuade or Advise

Exam Practice **Q4** Read the following extract from an advice leaflet about an election.

It's Decision Time — But Who Do I Vote For?

Unless you've been living under a rock for the past month, you'll probably have noticed that there's an election coming up. Deciding who to vote for can be a daunting task, but it's also an important one. Luckily, there's plenty of help out there.

Firstly, you need to be well-informed on the principles and policies that each party stands for. If you start to feel overwhelmed by all the political lingo in their leaflets, don't panic — have a look online, where there are plenty of websites that break it down for you.

It's also a good idea to look into the candidates in your constituency. Whoever gets elected will represent you in parliament, so you'll want to vote for someone who has a strong voice, and who will stand up for what your area needs.

It's true — choosing who to vote for isn't easy. However, if you take the time to do a bit of research, you will be able to make the right decision for you.

The writer is trying to advise the reader about voting. How do they try to do this?

Exam Practice **Q5** Read the following letter to the editor of the *Daily Muncaster* local newspaper.

Dear Sir,

I was frankly horrified to read your article about the new soft drink 'Swampy Water' being served in the tuck shop at Muncaster Primary School. This dangerous fad for drinking green, slimy water is clearly idiotic.

Firstly, young children may become confused and think it acceptable to drink real swamp water. I know from my time in the Territorial Army that this would be an ill-advised and perhaps even fatal decision. Secondly, 'Swampy Water' is full of unhealthy sugar and additives — how else would it acquire that lurid green tinge? Finally, the drink is expensive, which means children don't have sufficient funds to purchase the normal, healthy snacks that any sane parent would endorse.

To conclude, it is my firm belief that 'Swampy Water' should be immediately removed from the tuck shop at Muncaster Primary School.

Yours faithfully,
Gerry Bowness

The writer is trying to argue that 'Swampy Water' should be banned.
How does he try to do this?

I'm rooting for Teresa Green — her policies woodwork for us all...

Whether it's arguing, persuading or advising, a text's purpose will have a big impact on the way the author writes. To get the most out of your revision, make sure you practise linking a text's purpose to the writer's use of language techniques.

Writer's Viewpoint and Attitude

Q1   Read these play reviews. Write down whether each attitude is **positive**, **negative** or **balanced**.

    a) This playwright's recent offerings on the London stage had established
        high expectations, but his latest "masterpiece" falls far short of that hype.   ....

    b) I have never left a matinee performance and rushed straight
        to the box office to buy a ticket for that evening. Until now.   ....

    c) I can't say I was dazzled, but I certainly wasn't disappointed.
        A pleasant evening, if not one to write home about.   ....

Q2   Draw lines to match the extracts below to the viewpoints they're expressing.

    a) *"I'd be loath to send one of my own children to one, but the idea of abolishing mixed sex schools entirely is simply absurd."*

    b) *"I've always considered mixed schools to be a barrier to educational progress. We should all stick with traditional segregation."*

    c) *"Mixed schools are clearly superior, but parents should have a choice."*

    d) *"The outdated concept of single-sex education has persisted for far too long. All education should be gender-blind."*

    i) Prefers mixed schools and thinks single-sex schools should be abolished.

    ii) Prefers mixed schools but thinks single-sex schools should still be an option.

    iii) Dislikes mixed schools but thinks they should be offered as an option.

    iv) Dislikes mixed schools and thinks all schools should be single-sex.

Q3   Summarise **one** thing that these two writers agree on, and **one** thing that they disagree on. Use evidence from the text to support your answer.

Source A Mobile phone disruptions in lessons are a nightmare for any teacher. Surely the best way to prevent this is simply to ban them from school entirely.	**Source B** I'm not about to suggest that students should be permitted to use mobiles during lessons, but I fail to see that any harm can be caused by allowing them during lunchtimes.

The writers agree that ....

....

....

The writers disagree that ....

....

....

Literature and Literary Non-Fiction

After trying these exam-style questions, use the boxes below to tick how well you think you've done.

Q4 Read the following extract from a novel.

> Annie went from room to room, shaking her head at the disarray. The house looked as if it had been burgled. In the living room, a bookcase had been thrown onto the floor, and paperbacks were scattered chaotically across the carpet. In the kitchen, the floor was a treacherous landscape of smashed crockery and broken glass.
>
> Annie frowned and headed cautiously up the stairs, following the crashing sounds into the master bedroom. Lucas stood with his back to her. His hair was a frantic mess, his movements manic as he pulled every item of clothing out of his wardrobe and launched them behind him. He was muttering frenetically under his breath.
>
> "Lucas," Annie said calmly. He span around, surprised by her presence. His wide eyes were wild, beads of sweat had appeared on his forehead and his cheeks were red.
>
> "I can't find it," he said. "I've looked everywhere. It's lost. They'll kill me."
>
> "Don't be ridiculous. They're not going to kick you out just because you've lost your key to the clubhouse," said Annie, her arms folded.
>
> "What would you know about it, Annie?" said Lucas, his eyes flashing in annoyance. "They're obsessed with not letting any outsiders in. If they find out I've lost it... I'm doomed. Finished. Condemned."

For questions worded like this, you need to explain how the writer has created effects in your answer.

What impressions do you get of Annie and Lucas from these lines?

Q5 Read the following texts about teaching.

19th-Century Speech

A schoolmaster must view himself always as a military officer. He must demand respect from his troops, give no ground and yield no position. If he is not thorough, poor discipline and wayward behaviour will surely ensue. When a schoolmaster allows himself to be seen as a friend, all respect is lost. Imparting a meaningful and comprehensive academic education will become impossible. A schoolmaster without control is like a dog without bite.

21st-Century Autobiography

As my sepia-toned school-days become steadily more indistinct, the stern face of Mr Wan remains as clear as day. Wan was a firm disciplinarian, and his strict laws meant that I spent much of my adolescent life languishing in detention. But despite the inevitable resentment I felt for him at the time, Mr Wan did give me a lasting education. Not, sadly, in his beloved Chemistry; but certainly in the priceless lesson of human decency. Though my teenage self was unable to see it, Wan listened to me.

Compare how the two writers convey their different attitudes to teaching.

You're writing a book? What a novel idea...

There's a lot to think about when you're reading literature or a literary non-fiction text — so many literary devices... On the plus side, that gives you loads to write about. Besides, the more you practise identifying this stuff, the easier it gets.

19th-Century Texts

Q1   Read the following passage, then answer the questions below.

> Each year, the two families reunite for an agreeable gathering, at which games and cards are played, lively discussions had and much happiness felt by all involved. As the head of the Spears family, Sir Edward frequently begins the proceedings with a short speech, after which his younger brother (whose daughter Catherine, due to her poor health, is often absent from proceedings) proposes a game of cards or croquet to begin the day. The Withers family are historically the victors in games of a physical bent, but owing to an untimely case of influenza on the part of young Albert Withers, the Spears family this year emerged triumphant in all games played.

a) How are Catherine and Sir Edward related?

....

b) Which family won the croquet game this year and why?

....

c) Write down a word or phrase from the text which shows that the families enjoy being together.

....

Q2   Read each of these 19th-century texts, then summarise the writers' viewpoints on the themes below.

> As a gentleman, I find myself honour-bound to bring this matter to your attention. Young ladies of elevated standing, such as Miss Elizabeth, should not be seen walking alone with young men such as Tom Heygate. I think only of her best interests when I warn you of the scandal that could arise from your daughter's association with a mere farmhand.

a) Social class

....

....

> An oppressive silence fills the vast rooms of this house of late: now that my dear Ernest is gone away, they suffer heartily from the absence of his joyful laughter. Regardless, I have done what is necessary, for at school he will learn all that he needs to succeed in life — for that, his foolish mother's heart will learn to endure the ache.

b) Sending children away to boarding school

....

....

19th-Century Texts

Q3   Read the following extract from a letter written in the 19th century.

> Dearest Sophia,
>
> I hope you know that, as your doting and loving mother, I only ever wish for your good. I do not write to you to chastise, but to beseech you to consider your future. When I heard from your sister that you have been involved in these ghastly 'votes for women' campaigns in London, I came over in a terrible swoon. My darling, a respectable young lady of your age and social standing should not be getting involved in this sort of common and, I daresay, dangerous display. I implore you, for your safety and your reputation, to stay away from these unpleasant protests. If you were, heaven forbid, to be arrested and disgraced, how do you imagine we would ever persuade a young man to marry you? And if you will not consider yourself, at least consider your poor mother. How do you imagine I would survive the shock?
>
> When I told young Mr Greaves he was deeply concerned, and hoped you would soon be home and away from the perils of the city. He remains, for his part, a very handsome and respectable bachelor. He has recently been promoted at the bank, and I know he would be delighted to receive a note of congratulations from you.

What do you think and feel about the writer's views on her daughter's behaviour?

Q4   Read the following extract from a speech written in the 19th century.

> Friends and colleagues, I must first describe my sincerest gratitude for your attendance here today; it is the greatest honour to welcome so many intellectuals into my humble home. Knowing you all to be wise and influential persons, I have asked you here in the hope that we will concur on an issue of great importance.
>
> Gentlemen, you cannot fail to have perceived the overwhelming number of illiterate and uneducated children amongst the poor in our fair city — for when Mother and Father must work in the factories from the break of day until the skies turn dark, who will spare a moment to teach poor Tommy his ABCs? And, lacking this simple knowledge, how can poor Tommy hope to liberate himself from the poverty and crime by which he is surrounded? In ignoring the plight of these small children, we condemn them to a life of hunger and want.
>
> My esteemed friends, the solution to these problems is but a simple one — we must turn our attentions to establishing a unified system of education in this country. I move that we petition our national Parliament to pass a law that will make mandatory a basic education in reading and writing for all young children, be they rich or poor.
>
> This may well be a long fight. Indeed, it may be a difficult fight; but our cause is just and for the greater good of all — and so we must, with all our hearts, persevere.

What do you think and feel about the writer's views on educating children?

After a difficult fight with this section, we've persevered to the end...

Yep, you read that right — this page marks the end of Section 2. Don't feel too disappointed though, as there are still four more lovely sections of questions after this one. Up next: a handy dandy section about structure and language.

      Section Two — Reading: Understanding Texts

Tone, Style and Register

Q1   Draw a line to match each sentence to the word that best describes its tone.

a) Forcing captive animals to perform tricks in zoos and circuses
is a repulsive and shameful practice that must not be tolerated!   **sentimental**

b) Investigators have recently confirmed that DNA found at the
scene of the burglary matches that of suspect Fergus Maybach.   **detached**

c) I had a riot helping out at the birthday party! Who would've
guessed that kids were the perfect audience for my magic tricks?   **angry**

d) As he stared across the bay where they had first met, he remembered
vividly the tinkle of her laughter and the floral scent of her hair.   **upbeat**

Q2   For each pair of sentences below, underline the sentence written in a formal register.

a) "Sorry! We don't take credit cards."
"Customers are advised that we do not accept credit cards."

b) "It is essential to ensure you have the correct tools before proceeding."
"Check you've got the proper kit to hand before you go any further."

c) "Rising debts? We've got the info you need to sort your finances out."
"If you have financial complications, contact our trained advisors."

*If Gareth knew about
one thing, it was style.*

Q3   The text below is taken from a travel journal.
Write down **three** pieces of evidence from the
text that show it has a conversational style.

> At this point I was starting to get a tad — how shall I put it? — cheesed
> off. It's one thing being patient, accepting the fact that things don't
> always go to plan and that now and then delays just happen. It's quite
> another to be told, after paying good money for a ticket to Town A, that
> for no good reason you're taking a little detour through Village B, River C
> and Swamp D. I was finding it more and more difficult to follow what I
> had figured was the local way of dealing with difficulties — smiling and
> pretending to find the grim industrial scenery interesting. It wasn't.

1) ....

2) ....

3) ....

Tone, Style and Register

Now have a go at these exam-style questions — they will help you to put your knowledge into practice.

Q4 Read the following extract from a short story.

> Konrad Kaminski whistled as he ambled along the lane, twirling his umbrella acrobatically as he went. Occasionally he played a game with himself, tossing the umbrella lightly in the air and catching it again without breaking his stride.
>
> It had been raining, but now the sun was shining triumphantly. The puddles on the road glittered like molten silver, and the grass on either side offered up a heady scent of warm, wet earth. Everything radiated spring and promised summer.
>
> It was hard to tell if Konrad Kaminski was absorbing this positivity, or if he too was emitting it. Either way, his pink cheeks and sparkling eyes would have told a passer-by that here was a man for whom anything was possible. And indeed, had this been suggested to him, Konrad Kaminski would have agreed wholeheartedly. For here he was, a reasonably young man in robust health, who had just come into a small fortune, and who had all the necessary intelligence and requisite enthusiasm to make that small fortune into a very large one.

How does the writer make the tone of these lines upbeat and positive?

Q5 Read the following extract from an adventure holiday brochure.

> If you're up to your neck in revision, the promise of a long summer holiday might be the only thing keeping you going. For most students, the dream will be of lazy days spent with mates, maybe playing video games, or getting a bit of a tan down the park. There's nothing wrong with wanting a break. You've earned it. But here at Adventure Action, we can give you the chance to do something unforgettable with your summer.
>
> If you're aged 15 to 18, you could spend four weeks on one of our incredible adventure and conservation programmes at breathtaking locations around the world. You could trek through dense rainforest in Peru, to help build primary schools in isolated villages. You could take a flight over ancient glaciers to volunteer at a remote bear sanctuary in Alaska. Or you could earn a scuba-diving certificate whilst working in a marine biology lab in The Bahamas. Our programmes are tailored to give you a fantastic experience, where you can bag loads of new skills and be a part of something important.
>
> **Adventure beyond the usual this summer. Apply to Adventure Action today.**

How does the writer create a style that appeals to a young audience?

That's the problem with my jokes — they always lower the tone...

When you're reading a text, remember that its tone, style and register have all been carefully chosen by the writer in order to have the maximum impact on the reader. Nothing in a text is random. Unlike platypuses. They're very random.

Words and Phrases

Q1   Write the words in the box into the correct columns in the table.

Adjectives	Adverbs
threatening	

~~threatening~~	phenomenal
boastfully	contemptuous
lovely	bitterly
tragically	devotedly

Q2   What does the word 'sneered' suggest in this sentence?

> "Congratulations, Madge," Angus sneered.

....

....

Q3   How does the writer's choice of words create a different impression in each of the sentences below?

> "Just go," she whispered.

> "Just go," she spat.

....

....

....

Q4   How does the author use words and phrases to influence the reader in the sentence below?

> As my dear friend, I am sure you will understand my decision.

....

....

....

....

Words and Phrases

If you're hot on the trail of some exam-style practice, then look no further than the juicy questions below.
Afterwards, you can use the boxes at the bottom to say how confident you're feeling with words and phrases.

 Q5 Read the following extract from a short story.

> The wind rose suddenly. It was a bitter wind, a stinging wind, a wind that drowned all thoughts in a roaring cacophony of noise and fury. It was a tempest that barged across the barren, open moorland and threw itself against the stoic stone walls of the cottage. We didn't know when there would be an end to its howling or its persistent, unruly attempts to gain entry into our little home.
>
> We fought back the best we knew how. We had already nailed boards against the window shutters to stop them being wrenched open by the gusts; now we rolled up old rags and laid them against the gaps in the door frames to resist the draughts. Still it savaged us.
>
> "It can't get much worse, can it?" I asked Father, raising my voice above the roar of the enemy outside. His eyebrows drew together sternly.
>
> "We're just going to have to sit it out," he said. "We don't have any alternative."

How does the writer use words and phrases to show the effect of the weather?

 Q6 Read the following extract from a piece of fiction.

> She raised an eyebrow at him icily. Her mouth was a stern, straight line. It did not twitch.
>
> "Please," he pleaded, "it was a mistake. It won't happen again."
>
> Her silence was stone cold. He began to wring his hands fretfully. He could feel the sweat prickling like needles on the back of his neck. The seconds crawled by excruciatingly as he waited for her to say something, anything. He briefly considered speaking, but was too fearful of aggravating her further.
>
> "Evidently," she said at last, "you can no longer be trusted." The only emotion in her voice was disdain.
>
> His breath caught painfully in his chest; he knew the worst was coming.
>
> "I have no use for people I cannot trust," she continued. "You are dismissed. Leave now. Resign your post. Never let me see your face again. Understood?"
>
> Trembling, he managed a clumsy nod.
>
> "Good. Now get out."
>
> He turned and, dragging his feet like a condemned man, left the room.

How does the writer use words and phrases to present the characters in this passage?

Words have power — sadly, not the same kind of power as Superman...

The trick here is to get inside the mind of the writer. Writers know what impression they want to create, so they choose their words carefully. If you can work out what effect the writer was aiming for, it's easier to analyse their language.

Metaphors, Similes and Analogy

Q1   Write 'S' next to the similes and 'M' next to the metaphors below.

    a) She was a fraying cable of tension and anger, which could snap at any moment. ....

    b) The glassy eye of the lake watched us in silent judgement. ....

    c) Like a flock of tired ducks, we clustered around our teacher,
    who had brought us snacks to keep us going on the journey. ....

    d) His eyes were hot coals, burning fiercely at the vision he saw before him. ....

Q2   Use the words in the box to complete the following sentence about analogies.

non-fiction	compares	persuade	images

An analogy .... one thing to another. It uses memorable ....

to make something easier to understand. Analogies are often used in ....

texts to try to .... the reader about something.

Q3   Read the texts below. How does the use of an analogy in the second text make it more effective?

A running tap wastes around 6 litres of water for every minute it's left running.	*A running tap wastes the equivalent of seventeen cups of tea for every minute it's left running.*

....

....

Q4   What impression of the sky is the writer trying to create with the metaphors below?

> *The night sky was a cloth of violet silk scattered with gemstones.*

....

....

....

Metaphors, Similes and Analogy

 Q5 Read the following extract from a leaflet about health.

Driving towards a healthier you

If you had a Ferrari, I can only imagine that you would take good care of it. You might only fill its tank with premium fuel. You might have it regularly serviced. You would take pride in it, polish it at the weekends and keep the upholstery clean.

If you would take this much care of a Ferrari, surely you should take this much care of your body? After all, it's the only one you're ever going to have — you can't just trade this engine in if it breaks down. This means you should fuel yourself properly, eating regular meals that are full of the vitamins and minerals needed for optimum human performance. Keep your body's systems working effectively by exercising regularly and getting plenty of fresh air. And finally, take pride in your body: if you're striving to be happy and healthy, that is something to celebrate.

Regardless of shape or size, your body is priceless — and that's more than you can say for a luxury sports car, isn't it?

The writer is trying to persuade us to take care of our bodies.
How does he use analogy to do this?

 Q6 Read the following extract from a piece of fiction.

The landscape was dull steel. The sea was grey, the sky was grey and the mountains in the distance were grey. And we were grey too. Our meagre rations of bread and nameless slop had left us sallow-faced, with dark rings under our eyes. We huddled together nervously, like mice in a cage. A thin layer of snow carpeted the tundra already. The wind whipped at our cheeks and we shivered.

The soldiers were smoking by the hut, casting sideways glances at us once in a while, to make sure that we weren't doing anything foolish, like trying to escape. Eventually they trampled on their cigarettes and marched over to us — wolves in military uniform, coming to snarl at lambs.

"There's work to do!" the officer in charge barked, clapping his gloved hands and then gesturing to the crates we'd unloaded. "Come on! Get a move on!" He fired his orders like cannon balls, and we dispersed frantically to do as he said. "If they're not all unpacked by nightfall, no one eats."

How does the writer use metaphors and similes
to show the difficult conditions for the prisoners?

Sometimes, revising is like banging your head against a brick wall...

Get the differences between similes, metaphors and analogies clear in your mind. Once you know what you're looking for, it becomes much easier to spot them in texts — but always remember to comment on how they affect the reader.

Personification, Alliteration and Onomatopoeia

Q1 For each extract, circle the technique being used.
Then explain **one** effect that the technique creates.

Kat's ice cream was begging to be eaten.

© iStock.com/unalozmen

a) "The computer grumbled into life, before smugly informing
me that it was starting on six hours of updates."

Personification / alliteration / onomatopoeia

....

....

....

b) "The buzz and chatter of the students ruined the tranquillity of the scene."

Personification / alliteration / onomatopoeia

....

....

c) "Bag a Bargain at Brigson's — Portsmouth's Premier Pig Farm!"

Personification / alliteration / onomatopoeia

....

....

Q2 Underline **one** example of personification and **one** example of alliteration
in this advert, then explain their effect on the reader on the lines below.

A Call for Heroic Hikers!

Are you a fearsome fell-runner? Or maybe you just enjoy long strolls
through the hills? Whatever your ability, we want you to sign up for our
40-mile Wilderness Walk, taking place in the mountainous forest above
Tennerton. If you train hard, you'll not only get fit, but triumph over a
challenging foe and raise lots of money for charities in the local area.
To answer the cry of the hills and get involved, visit the council's website.

© iStock.com/peangdao

Effect of personification: ....

....

Effect of alliteration: ....

....

Personification, Alliteration and Onomatopoeia

And now, here's some handy exam-style practice for writing about these three language techniques.

Q3   Read the following extract from a short story.

> It was dark in the forest, and eerily close. Even small sounds were amplified into threatening noises. They heard the sinister creaking of the branches; the furtive rustle of leaves; the cracking of a twig that set their hearts racing. And every time they looked behind them, they were sure the scene had changed. Had that fallen log been there before? Had they really not seen that stream? It was as if the forest was playing tricks on them — purposefully trying to deceive and confuse them. Shadows seemed to shift, skipping about the forest floor, delighted at the predicament of the lost wanderers.
>
> Suddenly they heard a shrill screech. It pierced their ears and stopped them dead. The noise rang out again and they squinted upwards to see a large but haggard owl perching on a branch, staring down threateningly. It was guarding the path ahead.

How does the writer use onomatopoeia and personification to make these lines tense and dramatic?

Q4   Read the following extract from a piece of travel writing.

> The streets of Kuala Lumpur are a labyrinth of lost lanes, back-streets, dead-ends and alleys, which twist and turn and double back on themselves, constantly trying to bewilder the unaccustomed traveller. An apparently infinite series of haphazard side streets break out from the main street of the Chinatown area, like snakes winding across the desert. On every corner hang the pungent but irresistible smells of food stalls offering a cornucopia of exotic cuisines. Heavy trucks rumble past impatiently, whilst thousands of scooters whine and buzz like a swarm of bees, honking horns and hurling out exhaust fumes that stubbornly stagnate in the desperately hot air. The heat is relentless. Even standing still in the shade I can feel the sweat gathering on my forehead.
>
> In search of a bit of peace from the incessant heat and choking fumes, I make my way to the city centre park. Here, neat pathways wind their way leisurely through immaculate green lawns. On every side of the park, glimmering steel skyscrapers tower into the sky, peering down at the people walking below. It's like being surrounded by a giant metal rainforest, thronging with life.

How does the writer use alliteration, onomatopoeia and personification to create a vivid scene for the reader?

The workbook eyed me scoldingly, nagging me to get on with revision...

Whenever you're looking at a piece of descriptive writing, whether it's from a work of fiction or non-fiction, you're bound to find a few examples of these literary devices. Some, like onomatopoeia, you probably use yourself without even noticing.

Irony and Sarcasm

Q1 Use the words in the box to complete the following passage about irony and sarcasm.

> offence   intended   humour   opposite   cruel   context

Irony is when a piece of writing says the .... of its .... meaning.

The reader can tell that the writer is being ironic because of the .... Irony is

often used to add .... to a text. Sarcasm, on the other hand, is intended to cause

.... It uses irony with a .... tone to make fun of someone or something.

Q2 Tick which of the extracts below is sarcastic, then give an example and explanation to support your answer underneath.

> Ivan is a responsible lad with a keen sense of innovation. He's not afraid to embrace change, and he takes action where necessary without needing constant support. He can be forgetful at times, but overall he looks to be a worthy addition to the company.

☐

> Oh yeah, Ivan is a brilliant secretary — I especially appreciate the way he keeps forgetting to bring a pen and steals mine instead. And he's reorganised our files into a brand new system, which only he can understand — that's really made our lives easier.

☐

....

....

....

Q3 How does the writer use irony to show the characters' attitudes in the extract below?

> "You're so lucky to have made it as an actor," Gemma sighed.
> "You're well-paid, you travel the world, you meet all the celebrities..."
> Maya smiled. "It's a trial, that's for sure."
> "Oh yes, you clearly suffer for your art!" Gemma laughed.

....

....

....

....

Irony and Sarcasm

Q4   Read the following extract from an opinion column in a newspaper.

SATISFACTION GUARANTEED!

The other day I had to phone up my insurance company with the horrendously complicated problem of changing my address. After spending twenty thrilling minutes on hold, listening to a variety of boy bands performing their classic hits, I finally got through to the man on whom my lofty ambition rested — Brendan.

However, there was a slight hitch. It seems that, for such a highly skilled telephone operative as young Brendan, a task which may appear simple to us mere mortals must in fact be performed with studious precision. Fortunately, his professionalism shone through as he kept me informed that some "stuff had gone weird". This was obviously of great comfort to me, as I watched night-time slowly approach and began to revise my plans for what was left of the week.

How does the writer use irony and sarcasm to convey their attitudes to their insurance company?

Q5   Read the following extract from a piece of fiction.

"Have a good time at Kirsty's!" Hafsa's father called from the car, as he dropped her off at my house.

"Oh, we'll have a great time," she said, but rolled her eyes at me as soon as her dad pulled away. It really was going to be a fun-filled night; we had maths homework, physics homework and French homework to do for the next day. Coming up to exams, it seemed like the fun never stopped.

We settled down on my bedroom floor with a bowl of popcorn for sustenance. Hafsa opened up the maths textbook and read aloud.

"Find the coordinates of the minimum point of the graphs of each of the following equations."

I groaned.

"Fantastic," Hafsa said, "a nice easy one to start one with. Thanks Miss Hayward, you're a real friend to students."

"Compassionate and fashionable," I said with a smirk. "Did you see what she was wearing today?"

"What, that medieval blouse thing? Very on trend." We both laughed.

How does the writer use irony and sarcasm to present Hafsa and Kirsty?

Sarcasm — some say it's the lowest form of wit...

Remember that irony is less condescending than sarcasm. Because sarcasm tends to be nasty, it says as much about the person using it as the person or thing it's directed towards — something to bear in mind when you're analysing texts.

Rhetoric and Bias

Q1   Draw lines to match each sentence to its technique.

a) Nothing is more disgusting than a mouldy sandwich.   **antithesis**

b) The sandwich, which had been in the fridge for
at least a fortnight, was disgustingly mouldy.   **parenthesis**

c) Far from the sandwich heaven I'd been hoping
for, I found myself in sandwich hell.   **hyperbole**

Q2   Underline **one** rhetorical technique in this passage. Then, on the lines
below, name the technique and explain the effect on the reader.

> *Who has not felt outraged at the injustice of the world when viewing images of
> child poverty? We live in a world where millions of children must battle with
> hunger, thirst and poor sanitation every day. Your donation, if you can find it in
> your heart to give one, will truly change these children's lives for the better.*

Technique: ....

Effect: ....

....

....

Q3   Explain why the following text is biased. Use
evidence from the text to support your answer.

> By far the best hobby for young people is the card game "cribbage". All
> young people from the ages of eight to eighteen adore playing cribbage.
> It's easy to learn, doesn't need much equipment and provides hours of fun.

....

....

....

....

Rhetoric and Bias

If you need to write about rhetoric or bias in your exam, these exam-style questions will help you prepare.

Q4 Read the following extract from a travel brochure.

> Everyone daydreams. When you're stuck in the office — dealing with tricky customers, struggling with spreadsheets, drinking tepid tea — have you ever dreamt of turning your back on the daily drudge and escaping on a luxury break? Well, look no further than Malliwest Holidays.
>
> Perhaps your perfect escape features breathtaking Arctic scenery? If so, let us take you on an adventure to Iceland. Here you can be astounded by the otherworldly Northern Lights; you can luxuriate in the world-famous volcanic hot springs; and you can embark on one of our expertly guided whale watching tours.
>
> Or perhaps your idea of adventure is a five-star African safari? Malliwest's safari camps in Kenya offer accommodation in lavish tent complexes, with stunning views over the national park and the services of expert wildlife rangers, who will bring you face to face with animals such as lions, zebra and gazelle.
>
> And if relaxation is what you need, then rest assured that our top-end, all-inclusive beach resorts will satisfy your every desire. From private, white, sandy beaches to stunning infinity pools; from complimentary cocktails to Michelin-starred dining facilities; from award-winning spas to no-expenses-spared suites; your every wish will be catered for by our dedicated, professional staff.
>
> We can't wait to welcome you on your well-deserved break.

The writer is trying to persuade the reader to buy a holiday with Malliwest Holidays. How do they use rhetorical devices to do this?

Q5 Read the following extracts.

19th-Century Letter	21st-Century Review
Dear Jane,	The room smelt like its window hadn't been opened for about a century. The wallpaper was peeling. The carpet was a battlefield between all sorts of suspicious stains. Given the state of the rest of the room, I doubted that the 'fresh' bedding was clean, but it was the mattress that really drew my attention — it was like something from a Victorian prison cell, barely a few inches thick.

19th-Century Letter
Dear Jane,
I have arrived at my lodgings in Ware. They are satisfactory, if not impressive — the room must once have been decorated in good taste, but alas, it is the good taste of a bygone age. Nevertheless, the room is clean, tidy and of a good size. As I had expected, the mattress was not of the standard I am accustomed to (nor, for that matter, was the limited refreshment offered by the kitchens), but for a short stay, it will suffice.

21st-Century Review
The room smelt like its window hadn't been opened for about a century. The wallpaper was peeling. The carpet was a battlefield between all sorts of suspicious stains. Given the state of the rest of the room, I doubted that the 'fresh' bedding was clean, but it was the mattress that really drew my attention — it was like something from a Victorian prison cell, barely a few inches thick.

Compare how the two writers convey their attitudes to their rooms.

Homework is the worst thing ever — students swear that's not hyperbole...

When I tell you that learning this stuff is really important, I'm not exaggerating. Understanding bias and the rhetorical devices on these pages will really help you to write specific (and impressive) analyses of texts. Sounds good to me.

Descriptive Language

Q1 In the extract below, underline **two** descriptive verbs and circle **two** examples of imagery.

> The air smelt of scorched grass. I could feel the blistering sun burning into my skin as I trudged slowly through the prickly, dry vegetation, the straps of my heavy bag cutting lines like knives into my drooping shoulders. In the distance, the air shimmered in waves with the heat. I felt as if I were underwater, constantly being pulled back by the tidal drag of the temperature.

Q2 Circle which extract is the better example of descriptive writing and explain your answer using examples from the text.

i)
> *My first football match was great. The sights and sounds were amazing.*

ii)
> *I remember my first football match so clearly: the sound of the fans as loud as ten jet engines; the emerald green pitch; and the buzzing, electric atmosphere. I'll never forget it.*

I think extract **i) / ii)** is the most descriptive because ....

....

....

Q3 Read the following extract from a short story.

> Percy hastened me through the marble hallway towards the ballroom. I could already hear the thumping of music and the hum of voices. As the golden doors were opened, the noise hit me like a wave. The room was thronged with hundreds of guests, and they were all joking, laughing, making introductions. Their voices wove together into a single, undulating buzz of talk. Beyond their voices was the exuberant playing of the live band; drums and saxophones adding bass and melody to the already throbbing noise. There were other sounds too — the clinking of glasses, the occasional popping of champagne corks followed by cheers.
>
> And the colours! The men were all in tuxedos, cutting sharp lines of white and black, while the women shimmered in silks of every colour — emerald and scarlet, gold and violet, azure and cerise. Lights glittered from the chandeliers, sparkling on the women's jewellery and the martini glasses and the silverware. The ballroom had become a never-ending kaleidoscope of wealth.

"The writer of this extract uses descriptive language very successfully. The reader really feels like they're at the party." To what extent do you agree with this statement?

I'll describe myself — good looking, smells of roses, voice like an angel...

A great description really makes a piece of writing. In your exam, try to comment on the effect of specific techniques — like similes, metaphors and descriptive words and phrases — as well as the overall impression that the description creates.

Narrative Viewpoint

Q1　For each extract below, write whether it uses a first-, second- or third-person narrator.

   a) We crouched behind the sofa, trembling with fear.　.....................................

   b) "I don't remember," she said, but a memory was stirring in her mind.　.....................................

   c) You hurry down the dark street, heart thudding, head spinning.　.....................................

Q2　Explain why using a first-person narrator is effective in the extract below. Use evidence from the text to back up your answer.

> They told me I was in safe hands. They told me I wouldn't feel a thing. And I knew I should believe them. But lying there on the operating table, with the nurses and doctors swarming around my head, all I could feel was terror. One of them grinned at me reassuringly, and I pasted a smile on my face in return, but inside I felt as if someone had filled my gut with ice.

....

....

....

....

Q3　Read the following extract from a short story.

> It is very late and the train is quiet. There are only four passengers in the carriage.
> The first is a young man in a smart but cheaply-made suit. He has just been to his first job interview and is nervously and repeatedly checking his mobile phone.
> The second passenger is a middle-aged woman with greying hair. She is propped up against a window, fast asleep. She has three jobs at the moment, and together they just about pay the bills, but she spends her life in a constant state of exhaustion.
> The final two passengers are a retired couple, who have just been to visit their young grandchildren. The woman is feeling glad that she and her husband live over an hour away, and aren't asked to babysit more often. Her husband is contemplating the game of golf he has planned tomorrow.
> None of the passengers in the carriage take much notice of one another. None of the passengers in the carriage are aware that a murder has been committed on their train, and that by the time they pull in at their destination, they will all be suspects.

   How does the writer use narrative viewpoint to bring the characters to life?

I know why they call it the first person — because I'm number one...

Alas, identifying if a text uses the first, second or third person is usually the easy part of the exam. The harder part is trying to understand *why* the author has chosen a particular viewpoint — you'll need to write about the effect that it has.

Structure — Fiction and Non-Fiction

Q1   Draw lines to match each structural technique with its definition.

a) **Non-linear writing**

b) **Perspective shifts**

c) **Linear writing**

i)   When the point of view of a text moves between different characters and/or locations.

ii) Writing that tells the events of a story in chronological order.

iii) Writing that tells the events of a story in a non-chronological order.

Proof that structure is important.

Q2   Read the extract below.

> It was one of those frosty winter mornings. The sky was a clear forget-me-not blue, and the grass stood rigid and silver with frost. Robins chirped proudly as they flittered in and out of the glittering bramble bushes. The kitchen sang with the smell of hot, buttered toast and fried bacon. A large, red pot of tea sat on the kitchen table, steam curling from its spout.

Cross out the incorrect word from each pair of bold words.

a) This extract opens with **description / dialogue**.

b) This means that the reader's focus is initially on the **setting / characters**.

c) It moves the reader's attention from **outside / inside** to **outside / inside**.

Q3   The purpose of the extract below is to advise. It has been structured into paragraphs. On the lines below, explain how the paragraphs help the text to achieve its purpose.

> Trying to de-clutter your life? Don't worry — we've got all the tips and tricks you need!
> Firstly, set yourself a target. Whether it's cutting down your wardrobe by half, or filling a specific box with cast-offs, having a clear goal in mind will help you to de-clutter efficiently.
> When you've decided on a target, it's time to get de-cluttering! Enlist your friends and family so that it's not too boring a chore, and you'll be finished with the job in no time.
> It's a tough task, but just think how great you'll feel when your life is as clean and clutter-free as can be.

....

....

....

Structure — Fiction and Non-Fiction

Q4 This is the ending to a short story. Joan is eighty-six years old, and one of the nurses from her care home has volunteered to take her to the beach.

> They arrived shortly before lunchtime. The seagulls squawked noisily overhead, bright as doves against the blue sky. The nurse pushed the wheelchair down the boardwalk. Looking out over the sand and the grey-green sea, Joan was transfixed.
>
> The first time she had been to the beach was as a little girl, shortly before the war broke out. It had been a hot day. The beach was full of people sprawled on multicoloured deck chairs and picnic blankets, lending the scene a carnival feel. She remembered the smell of the water as she raced into the sea for the first time. She remembered the feeling of damp sand between her fingers and toes, and how the sea salt had dried into tiny crystals on her skin. Her mother had packed a picnic of hard-boiled eggs and potato salad. It had been the best day of her life so far, and as her father had bundled her into a towel, tired and sun-soaked, ready to go home, she had already been looking forward to the next visit.
>
> Now Joan watched the children race delightedly across the sand like she had done. Her nurse bought her fish and chips for lunch. Joan bought sticks of rock for her great-grandchildren. As the sun was going down, and they headed back to the car, Joan looked back over her shoulder. She knew there wouldn't be a next visit — but she didn't mind. She had seen the sea again.

How has the writer used structure to make these lines interesting for the reader?

Q5 Read the following extract from a newspaper article.

BAKING AND BONDING

After a week spent with my grandma, participating in the gentle, unhurried life of a retiree, I've come to a conclusion: we should all be baking more.

There's nothing quite as relaxing as baking. The therapeutic act of beating the eggs and the sugar together in a sturdy bowl; the anticipation as you wait for it to bake — what better way to unwind?

Baking can provide an invaluable bonding opportunity, too. Last week, I got to spend some quality time with my granny, as we bickered over which order to mix in the ingredients and swapped secrets for getting the perfect bake.

In the modern world, some may argue that there's no time for the domestic pursuits of yesteryear — why bother, when 24-hour supermarkets will sell us whatever we like, whenever we like it?

Well, as Granny and I can attest, sometimes it's best to take a break from the pressures of modern life. And if, in the process, you end up with a delicious batch of home-cooked goodies... well, that's just the icing on the cake.

The writer is trying to persuade us to bake more.
How do they use structural features to achieve this?

This workbook is structured so that you ace your exams...

Both fiction and non-fiction texts are structured for maximum effect. Non-fiction is often structured to make its content clear, or to have a persuasive effect. Fiction can be structured to engage the reader in its events, settings or characters.

Sentence Forms

Q1   Label each sentence below as either simple, compound or complex.

a) Gazing longingly out to sea, the sailor dreamed of adventure.   ....

b) I waited for an hour, but he never arrived.   ....

c) She listened in shock to the news on the radio.   ....

d) He never imagined that people could live in such poverty.   ....

e) The sun rose reluctantly, casting sombre shadows across the fields.   ....

f) Night was closing in fast, so we needed to find the path soon.   ....

Q2   The four sentences below say a similar thing in different ways.

a) | *Bullying in schools is a severe problem.* |

c) | *Haven't you had enough of bullying?* |

b) | *Stop bullying today.* |

d) | *We must stop bullying!* |

For each sentence, identify the type of sentence using the options in the box, then explain why a writer might have chosen each one. The first answer has been done for you.

| statement | exclamation |
| question | command |

a) Sentence type: ....*statement*....

Using a clear statement makes the writer sound sincere and objective. The writer might have chosen

to use a statement to emphasise that bullying is a serious topic.

b) Sentence type: ....

....

....

c) Sentence type: ....

....

....

d) Sentence type: ....

....

....

Sentence Forms

Make sure you're prepared to write about sentence forms with these exam-style questions.

 Q3 Read the following extract from a piece of fiction.

> The theatre hummed with expectant conversation as the spectators began to fill the stalls. The red velvet seats and gentle golden lighting gave the impression of being caught in the centre of a giant ruby. There was a magical feeling, as if everyone knew they were going to witness something spectacular that night, and eyes kept flickering over to the theatre drapes, wondering when the show would begin.
>
> Backstage, biting his fingernails down to the nail-bed, was the one they were all waiting for. Mikhail had been told by everyone he met that he was the greatest tenor of all time. Conductors had shed a tear when he sang, audiences had wept openly. But that never stopped him from feeling sick with nerves before a performance. What if his voice faltered? What if he forgot the words? What if he disappointed them all?
>
> "Sixty seconds to curtain," the stage manager called to him. Mikhail took a deep breath. His palms were damp with sweat. His legs felt like jelly. He didn't know if he was ready for this.

How has the writer used different sentence forms to make these lines tense and dramatic?

 Q4 Read the following extract from a piece of fiction.

> The shot rang out. Jane powered off the blocks. The sound of the stadium had faded now, and only one thing mattered: putting one foot in front of the other, faster than she had ever done before. This was her race. She was born for this! Her blood pounded in her ears as she sprinted round the track.
>
> In the distance, the finish line was approaching. There were still two runners ahead of her. Faster! Jane urged herself on. Her legs burned. Her lungs screamed. But she was gaining on them. She overtook one. Still faster! At the last second, she overtook the final competitor and her foot came down first, landing triumphantly over the white line.
>
> Jane slowed to a halt, and doubled over with her hands on her knees as she gasped for breath. Wiping the sweat from her eyes, she looked up again at the stadium, and nearly cried with joy. Thousands and thousands of people were on their feet, cheering; they were waving flags and calling her name, smiles reaching from ear to ear. She could hardly believe it. All the months of hard training had paid off and she had achieved her lifelong dream: she had won a gold medal at the Olympics.

How has the writer used different sentence forms to describe Jane's experience?

"And your sentence shall be — two hours of revision! Mwah ha ha..."

Sentences might seem easy enough, but they're fundamental to a piece of writing. It's worth taking the time to perfect your skills at analysing them closely. Ask yourself *why* the sentence has been written like it has, and think about its effects.

 [ ]   [ ]   [ ]

Presentation

Q1   Explain the effect of presenting the material below as a numbered list.

> Here's your easy guide to starting a rose garden:
> 1. Pick a spot that gets plenty of sunlight.
> 2. Prepare your soil — make sure it's at the right acidity level for your roses.
> 3. Plant the roses.
> 4. Water as required. The soil should be moist at all times.

....

....

Q2   Label this newspaper article with the correct terms from the box, and explain the effect of each feature on the lines underneath.

> subheading
>
> headline
>
> picture

a) Feature: ....

Effect: ....

....

....

....

b) Feature: ....

Effect: ....

....

....

....

c) Feature: ....

Effect: ....

....

....

....

VILLAGE HALL VILLAIN

Details emerged last night of a crime that has rocked the small village of Chirlton-upon-Clye.

A large amount of money, which had been raised as part of a charity event, was stolen from the village hall in the early hours of Monday morning.

Chirlton-upon-Clye

New suspect

CCTV evidence has revealed the presence of a young woman dressed in black clothing at the scene of the crime.   Police have thus far been unable to trace the woman, who they are now considering the prime suspect in the case.

Local outrage

Local residents have reacted angrily to the theft.

"It makes me sick knowing that there are people willing to steal from this community," said Cath Norton, who lives opposite the village hall. "This incident has threatened our safety, our way of life, and our community spirit."

Information appeal

Police are appealing for any residents with more information to contact them immediately.

Presentation

Q3   Read the following extract from a newspaper article.

SAVE OUR CYCLISTS

We've become ever more aware of the impact our cars are having on the environment, and the number of bicycles on the roads has rocketed accordingly. So why aren't our roads better adapted for cyclists?

Dangerous and deadly

Every year, tens of thousands of cyclists are injured in road-related accidents. I believe this is due, in part, to a lack of dedicated cycle lanes — meaning larger, faster vehicles are not kept at an adequate distance on busy and dangerous roads.

Time to change

It's ludicrous that our roads have not been adapted to the changing habits of those who use them.

I'm starting a campaign to lobby for government funding, in order to create more cycle lanes throughout the nation's road network. Together, we can make our roads safer for all.

The writer is trying to persuade the reader to agree with their point of view. How do they use presentational devices to do this?

Q4   Read the following extract from a piece of travel writing.

Isla Vente

An Island Paradise

The island boasts idyllic, secluded beaches

Isla Vente is a beautiful, mountainous island, which early settlers nicknamed "the Green Jewel" thanks to the lush forests that carpet the island's eastern side.

Divers can explore beautiful unspoilt coral reefs

The beaches on Isla Vente are beautiful in appearance, with glistening white sand and pristine blue seas. They are some of the most secluded and unspoilt beaches in the world. For swimming and sunbathing they provide the most calming and leisurely experience available. The beaches also provide incomparable surroundings for diving, snorkelling, and other water sports.

The writer is trying to inform and persuade the reader. How do they use presentational devices to do this?

Presentation is important, so turn up to your exam in your best suit...

When you're writing about presentational devices, it's crucially important to explain the effect they have — it's not enough to just describe the presentational device itself. Stick to the P.E.E.D. structure and you can't go far wrong.

Section Three — Reading: Language and Structure

Writing with Purpose

Q1   Put each of the following writing techniques into the appropriate column of the table, depending on whether they're more common in informative or persuasive writing.

an impersonal tone	rhetorical questions	technical terms	emotive language

Informative writing	Persuasive writing

The leader of the 'no to school uniforms' campaign was a formidable opponent.

Q2   Complete this brief plan to show how you would structure a speech arguing in favour of school uniforms.

Introduction: *Clearly state viewpoint and outline the main points of the argument.*

1) ....

2) ....

3) ....

Conclusion: ....

Q3   Rewrite the informative text below so that it persuades the reader to visit the church.

Lyttlewich Church

Situated in the rural village of Lyttlewich, Howtonshire, Lyttlewich Church is one of the oldest churches in the country: some parts of the church were built in 984 AD. The church receives thousands of visitors a year, and is particularly renowned for its artwork, which has recently been restored.

....

....

....

....

....

Writing with Purpose

If you've mastered those short questions, here are some exam-style questions to have a crack at.
When you're done, tick a box at the bottom of the page to show how you got on with the whole lot.

 Q4 Answer the exam-style question below.

> One of your classmates has said that going to bed early is a waste of time, as all worthwhile television programmes are on late at night.
>
> You have decided to write a speech to persuade your class to agree with your views on this idea. You could write for or against the idea.
>
> **Write a compelling speech giving your views.**

 Q5 Answer the exam-style question below.

> Your school have said that creative subjects such as Art and Drama should be compulsory for all students aged 5-16.
>
> You have decided to write a speech to be given to your school governors to share your views on this idea. You could argue in favour or against this idea.
>
> **Write an engaging speech giving your views.**

 Q6 Answer the exam-style question below.

> *In this question you will be assessed for the quality*
> *of your **creative prose writing** skills.*
>
> Choose **one** of the following titles for your writing:
>
> **Either,** *(a)* The Bike Race.
> **Or,** *(b)* The Dilemma.
> **Or,** *(c)* Write about a time when you forgot something important.
> **Or,** *(d)* Write a story which begins:
>   I couldn't shake the feeling that I'd been here before...

Purr, puss... there's a joke in there somewhere...

It's really important to keep your purpose in mind when you're answering the writing questions in each paper. As part of your exam preparation, practise spotting the purpose in these questions, then adapting your writing to match.

Writing for an Audience

Q1 Rewrite each sentence below so that it's appropriate
for an audience who have no expertise on the subject.

a) "Fertilisers provide phosphorus and potassium, which are essential for plant growth."

Fertilisers provide things that plants need to grow.

b) "The ossicle bones in the ear (the malleus, incus and stapes)
are some of the smallest in the human skeleton."

....

c) "Roman legionaries used javelins and throwing-darts to defeat their enemies."

....

Q2 Write down a good opening sentence for each of the texts below.
Make sure it's suitable for the audience given in the question.

a) An article for a teenage magazine, in which you say that schools should
spend more time teaching students how to manage their money.

....

....

b) A leaflet to be given out at your local health centre advising adults about healthy eating.

....

....

Q3 The extract below is from a letter written to a close friend.
Rewrite it on the lines below as if you were writing to a local newspaper.

> The fresh fruit in the shops around here is rubbish.
> You can't find a decent apple for love nor money!

....

....

....

Writing for an Audience

 Q4 Answer the exam-style question below.

> *In this question you will be assessed for your ability to write* ***creative prose*** *for a general, adult audience.*
>
> Choose **one** of the following titles for your writing:
>
> **Either,** *(a)*   The Boat Trip.
> **Or,** *(b)*   Finding My Roots.
> **Or,** *(c)*   Write about a time when you got lost.
> **Or,** *(d)*   Write a story which begins:
>   It was an ordinary Wednesday morning when it happened...

 Q5 Answer the exam-style question below.

> Your headteacher believes that young people are often unaware of the dangers they face when crossing roads.
>
> **Write a magazine article aimed at students in your year group suggesting ways they can keep safe when crossing roads.**
>
> You could include:
> • an explanation of the dangers that roads can pose;
> • your ideas about how to keep safe while crossing roads.

 Q6 Answer the exam-style question below.

> Imagine you have just been on holiday.
>
> You have decided to write a review of the destination you visited, to be published in a travel guide aimed at young adults.
> You could write positively or negatively about the destination.
>
> **Write a lively review sharing your opinions about the destination.**

I hypnotise my audience to keep their attention...

You are feeling sleepy... very sleepy... and on the count of three, you'll be able to answer every question in this book with great ease... Ah, if only it were that simple. Sadly, the only way to get the hang of writing questions is to practise. Lots.

Creative Writing

Q1 Use the words in the box to complete the following sentences about how to begin a piece of creative writing.

attention   middle   clichés   character   engage   direct

Creative writing needs to immediately .... the reader.

This is often achieved by starting in the .... of the

action or by introducing an unusual .... Creative

writing can also use .... address to grab the reader's

.... — but it needs to avoid ....

By the sixteenth read-through, Clara's favourite story was starting to grate on Ron.

Q2 Imagine you are going to write a piece of creative writing about somebody who's lost in a forest.

a) What narrative viewpoint would you use? Give a reason for your answer.

....

....

b) Write down two descriptive adjectives you could use, and explain their effect.

....

....

c) Write down a simile you could use.

....

Q3 Write the closing sentences for each of the texts below.

Remember that the ending of a piece of creative writing needs to leave an impression on the reader.

a) A story about a spaceship that crashes on an alien planet.

....

....

b) A story set on a desert island.

....

....

Creative Writing

Time to put all that short practice... into practice. Here are some exam-style questions to sink your teeth into.

Q4 Answer the exam-style question below.

---

*In this question you will be assessed for the quality of your **creative prose writing** skills.*

Choose **one** of the following titles for your writing:

Either, *(a)* The Gang.
Or, *(b)* The Glass Staircase.
Or, *(c)* Write about your local area.
Or, *(d)* Write a story which begins:
I should never have taken the long way home...

Q5 Answer the exam-style question below.

---

*In this question you will be assessed for the quality of your **creative prose writing** skills.*

Choose **one** of the following titles for your writing:

Either, *(a)* The Penguin.
Or, *(b)* Flying Home.
Or, *(c)* Write about a time when you went shopping.
Or, *(d)* Write a story which begins:
I'd never met anybody like her before...

Q6 Answer the exam-style question below.

---

*In this question you will be assessed for the quality of your **creative prose writing** skills.*

Choose **one** of the following titles for your writing:

Either, *(a)* Changing the World
Or, *(b)* The New Book
Or, *(c)* Write about a train journey.
Or, *(d)* Write a story which begins:
There was simply no other option...

Are you sitting comfortably? Then I'll begin...

Don't underestimate paper 1, section B — it's tempting to think it's less important than Section A, but it's worth as many marks as all of the reading questions put together. Use your imagination to write something that really stands out.

More Creative Writing

Q1 Rewrite the passage below, replacing the underlined words with more interesting descriptive vocabulary.

> The <u>long</u> branches of the <u>tall</u> tree <u>moved</u> in the wind, <u>dropping</u> leaves all over the <u>green</u> grass underneath.

....

....

....

Q2 Use descriptive imagery to write a sentence about each of the things below.

a) An old car.

....

b) An urban landscape.

....

c) The feeling of embarrassment.

....

Q3 In the box below, create a plan for a story with the title 'The Castle'.

You could plan your story in different ways, e.g. you could do a written plan or a spider diagram.

More Creative Writing

Don't close your creative writing bag o' tricks yet... these exam-style questions are just waiting to be lit up by your vocabulary. Have a go, then tick a box at the bottom of the page to show how you got on.

 Q4 Answer the exam-style question below.

> *In this question you will be assessed for the quality of your* **creative prose writing** *skills.*
>
> Choose **one** of the following titles for your writing:
>
> **Either,** *(a)* The New Girl.
> **Or,** *(b)* Growing Up.
> **Or,** *(c)* Write about an interesting building.
> **Or,** *(d)* Write a story which begins:
> There were only two ways they could have known about the secret...

 Q5 Answer the exam-style question below.

> *In this question you will be assessed for the quality of your* **creative prose writing** *skills.*
>
> Choose **one** of the following titles for your writing:
>
> **Either,** *(a)* Reaching New Heights.
> **Or,** *(b)* The Storyteller.
> **Or,** *(c)* Write about a time when you felt happy.
> **Or,** *(d)* Write a story which begins:
> It was the fourteenth time it had happened this week...

 Q6 Answer the exam-style question below.

> *In this question you will be assessed for the quality of your* **creative prose writing** *skills.*
>
> Choose **one** of the following titles for your writing:
>
> **Either,** *(a)* The Broken Window.
> **Or,** *(b)* Going Camping.
> **Or,** *(c)* Write about a time when you felt guilty.
> **Or,** *(d)* Write a story which begins:
> There was no explanation for what I had just seen...

Just don't get too kre8tiv with your spelling...

For really interesting, vivid writing, you need to <u>show</u> the reader what's going on instead of just <u>telling</u> them. E.g. instead of writing "Ajay was excited", you could write: "Ajay's eyes were bright, and his stance was upright and eager."

Writing Articles

Q1 Read the exam question and then answer the questions below.

> Your friend has said that students should be allowed time off for all religious holidays, not just Christmas and Easter.
>
> You have decided to write an article for your school newspaper to share your views on this idea. You could write in favour or against this idea.

a) What is the purpose and who are the audience in this question?

Purpose: ....   **Audience:** ....

b) Write a rhetorical question which you could use in this article.

....

c) Make up a believable fact or statistic which you could include.

....

Q2 Read the question below, then write a good opening sentence on the lines underneath.

> Your local Member of Parliament has said that the human race is not doing enough to protect the planet's endangered species.
>
> You have decided to write an article for a wildlife magazine to share your views on this idea. You could write in favour or against this idea.

....

....

Q3 Read the sentences below, then rewrite them so that they're suitable for an opinion column in a broadsheet newspaper.

Remember — opinion columns are generally written in a personal tone.

a) "Doctors have warned of the problems the nation faces if the number of smokers in this country does not decrease."

When it comes to smoking, the doctors' warnings are clear — we can't carry on like this.

b) "The government have today announced a policy that will see unsupervised children banned from public places."

....

c) "Temperatures soared across the country this weekend in an unprecedented heat wave."

....

Writing Articles

Q4 Read the following extract from a broadsheet newspaper article.

CRISIS FOR CLASSICAL MUSIC

A report released today by the RBMS (Royal British Music Society) claims that up to 50% of young people in Britain have never listened to a piece of classical music. A further 24% say that they have heard a piece of classical music, but 'would not choose' to listen to the genre.

The report, which was commissioned by the Society in response to a decline in attendance at many live concerts, has provoked concern amongst the musical fraternity, with many claiming that classical music could meet an untimely end if further action is not taken.

Luigi Piccolo, head of the world-renowned Royston Philharmonic Orchestra, said: "Over the next fifty years or so, we're going to become completely irrelevant. It's time to start appealing to a wider audience."

You have decided to write an opinion column to be published alongside this article, in which you share your views on the report.

Write an engaging article for the newspaper giving your views.

Q5 Answer the exam-style question below.

> Your local community leaders are concerned that active hobbies, such as sports, are falling by the wayside in favour of time spent using tablets or smartphones.
>
> **Write an article for your local newspaper advising people how to spend less time in front of screens and more time engaging in active hobbies.**
>
> You could include:
> • ideas for how to cut down on the use of tablets or smartphones;
> • examples of active hobbies to get involved in.

Q6 Answer the exam-style question below.

> You have read a newspaper article which states that travelling by boat is better than travelling by aeroplane.
>
> You have decided to write an article for a travel magazine in which you share your views on this idea. You could write in favour or against this idea.
>
> **Write an entertaining article giving your views.**

I fell asleep whilst reading that — must have been a snooze-paper...

Hopefully you're now feeling suitably in the know about writing articles. Don't forget that there are lots of different types of article, though — make sure you read the question carefully, and adapt your tone, language and style to match.

Writing Leaflets and Travel Writing

Q1 Use the words in the box to complete the following sentences about travel writing.

opinions	conversational	magazines	place	first	entertain

Travel writing is always about a specific .... It is commonly found in

.... and books. It is used to convey the writer's .... about

a place. Its purpose is often to .... It uses a .... tone

and is often written in the .... person in order to engage its audience.

Q2 Read the text below.

> Come to Caleb's Kitchen today, for:
> • Delicious, freshly made food.
> • A warm and welcoming environment.
> • And on top of all that, unbelievably low prices!

Caleb's plan to make the restaurant warm had backfired slightly.

a) Do you think this extract is from a leaflet or a piece of travel writing?

....

b) Write down a reason for your answer.

....

Q3 Read the exam-style question below, then write a suitable opening on the dotted lines.

> A local restaurant owner has said that fast-food chains make it difficult for independent restaurants to make any money, so they should be banned.
>
> **Write the text for a leaflet to be distributed in your local area giving your views on this idea. You could write in favour or against this idea.**

....

....

....

....

Writing Leaflets and Travel Writing

You'll know what's coming by now... yep, it's some exam-style questions to really test your talents.

 Q4 Read the following extract from a piece of travel writing.

> **This summer, my family and I found ourselves in a conundrum.** Two weeks into the summer holidays, we were already sick of visiting the same old places. With another month ahead of us, we decided to take action. After some research, we discovered Oakfall Island, a small island a few hours' drive up the coast.
>
> As it turns out, Oakfall Island is the perfect destination for a low-budget 'staycation'. We knew we were on to a winner when the kids loved the boat ride over from the mainland! The island itself did not disappoint — our campsite was fully equipped with clean shower blocks, a barbecue area and an adventure playground, and there were acres of open fields and forest for the kids to explore.
>
> With its ancient ruins and rolling hills, Oakfall Island truly has something for everyone. My wife loved exploring the small but perfectly formed local museum, and I found a reasonably priced restaurant that served the most delightful desserts I have ever tasted, as well as a small deli selling organic local produce.

Using details from this text, write the text for a leaflet in which you persuade the reader to visit Oakfall Island.

 Q5 Answer the exam-style question below.

> Some younger pupils at your school have said they are finding it difficult to decide which GCSE subjects they would like to study.
>
> You have decided to write a leaflet in which you advise students at your school about choosing their GCSEs.
>
> **Write the text for a leaflet giving advice about choosing GCSE subjects.**

 Q6 Answer the exam-style question below.

> You have read a leaflet for a tour company which says young people should travel and experience new cultures before they start their adult life.
>
> You have decided to write a piece of travel writing for a broadsheet newspaper in which you share your views on this idea. You could write in favour or against this idea.
>
> **Write an entertaining piece of travel writing giving your views.**

Finished these? Travel write on over to the next page...

There's a lot going on in these pages. These types of writing could pop up in that pesky exam, though, so you need to make sure you've got your head around the styles and techniques of both of them before you move on to the next page.

Writing Reports, Essays and Reviews

Q1   Read the extracts below. Draw lines to match each one to the correct form.

a)   In summary, the red-tailed bat does not appear to be at immediate risk of extinction. However, in light of its ineffectual breeding habits, it merits close monitoring by conservationists.

Report

b)   All in all, the exhibition was a remarkably charming insight into the fascinating world of the red-tailed bat. If you happen to have a spare hour or two this weekend, I'd say it's more than worth the £15 entry fee.

Review

Q2   Each of the extracts below is inappropriate for a report.
Rewrite each one so that it's appropriate for this form.

a)   "Some people agree with the idea of scrapping university fees, and some don't, so I'm not really sure what we should do."

....

....

b)   "The whole idea's complete twaddle, to be honest."

....

c)   "I really think we should invest in the new community centre!"

....

Q3   Read the question below, then write a brief plan to show how you would structure your answer.

You have read a report which says that we should stop exploring space, because it is too expensive and dangerous.
Write an essay in which you share your views on this idea.

Introduction: ....

1) ....

2) ....

3) ....

Conclusion: ....

Writing Reports, Essays and Reviews

 Q4 Read the letter below, written by a local resident to their MP.

> Dear Mr Yates,
>
> I write in order to urge you to take action on a fundamental matter. The glottalbug population in Brueton is rapidly declining; we simply must take steps to stop this.
>
> Glottalbugs are very important to our village's ecosystem: we need them to pollinate our crops, which is crucial in our agricultural community. Many jobs in the area are reliant on a good harvest; without the glottalbug, unemployment rates will soar.
>
> Unfortunately, the scale of the operation required to rescue our six-legged friends is a large one, and it's rather expensive. We will need support from the council to be able to fix this problem. Please help the glottalbugs, Mr Yates; you are their last chance.
>
> Yours sincerely,
>
> Mr D. Range.

Imagine you are the MP, Mr Yates. Write an essay, to be posted on your local council's website, in which you share your views on this problem.

 Q5 Answer the exam-style question below.

> It has been suggested that professional footballers are paid too much, so they should be legally required to donate a portion of their earnings to charity.
>
> **Write a report for the government to advise them on whether or not this idea should be put into action.**
>
> You could include:
> * the benefits of the idea;
> * the drawbacks of the idea.

 Q6 Answer the exam-style question below.

> Imagine you have just been to see a film.
>
> You have decided to write a review for your cinema's newsletter, in which you share your views on the film. You could write about it in a positive or negative way.
>
> **Write a lively review giving your opinion on the film.**

I've reviewed the situation, and I think it's time for another biscuit...

It's worth trying to answer some of these questions as if you were in an exam. Time yourself, and make sure there's nothing around to distract you. It's tough, but it'll pay off in the long run — you won't have a lot of time on the day.

Writing Speeches

Q1 Read the following bits of advice for speech writing and circle if they're true (T) or false (F).

a) Speeches should start with a dramatic statement and then slowly wind down. (T / F)

b) You should try to make your speech appropriate for reading out loud. (T / F)

c) If you're writing a speech, it can be helpful to address your audience directly. (T / F)

"Well helloooo Wembley!"

© iStock.com/muzon

Q2 You are writing a speech to encourage local residents to recycle more often. Write a sentence for the speech which uses each of the following language techniques.

a) Directly addressing the audience

As you all know, sometimes the effort of sorting out your recycling feels like a big waste of time.

b) A rhetorical question

....

c) An exclamation

....

d) A list of three

....

Ladies and Gentlemen, I declare that the time is right for some exam-style practice.

 Q3 Answer the following exam-style question.

> You have read a magazine article which says that pizza is too unhealthy, so it should be illegal to serve it to anyone under the age of eighteen.
>
> You have decided to write a speech to be delivered at a national conference of restaurant-owners to share your views on this idea. You could write in favour or against the idea.
>
> **Write an engaging speech giving your views.**

I'm making an easy Italian meal for dinner — it's a pizza cake...

The questions on this page should have made you feel more confident about writing speeches that have a strong impact on their audience. Try to make your speech memorable — you really need to be able to engage your audience here.

Writing Letters

Q1 Look at the extract from an exam-style question below, then fill in the table to give the purpose, audience and register of the letter.

> You have decided to write a letter to your local council to argue that there should be more facilities for teenagers in your local area.

Purpose	
Audience	
Register	(formal / informal)

Q2 How would you start and end letters to the following people? The first one has been done for you.

a) Your headteacher

Start: *Dear Ms Coombes* .... End: ....

b) Your best friend

Start: .... End: ....

c) Your local fire safety officer (you don't know their name)

Start: .... End: ....

Q3 Imagine you're writing a letter to your head of year to argue that year 11 should be provided with a common room. Write a short paragraph from this letter on the lines below.

....

....

....

....

Q4 Answer the following exam-style question.

> A proposal has been made to build more houses in rural areas.
>
> You have decided to write a letter to the editor of a local newspaper to share your views on this proposal. You could write in favour or against this proposal.
>
> **Write a compelling letter giving your views.**

I'm quite good at writing letters — A, Q, R, Z, F...

Don't worry if you get a question that asks you to write in a more modern form, like an email. Just make sure you adapt your writing to the audience and purpose in the question, and definitely avoid including any text speak or smiley faces.

Section Four — Writing: Creative and Non-Fiction

Paper 1 — Questions

In this section, <u>you</u> get to be the examiner. You'll look at some students' answers to exam questions and <u>decide what marks</u> they should get. It'll help you understand what the examiners are <u>looking for</u> — which will <u>improve</u> the quality of your answers. Here's how it works:

1) Read the sample exam questions and text on pages 62-65. They're similar in style to the ones you'll get in <u>paper 1</u> (called '20th Century Literature Reading and Creative Prose Writing').

2) You <u>don't</u> have to answer the questions. Instead, on pages 65-75 there are some <u>sample student answers</u> for you to <u>mark</u>.

3) For each question, we've given you a <u>mark scheme</u>. You can use this to decide <u>how many</u> marks each of the sample answers is worth.

Section A — Reading

Read lines 1-8.

A1.   List **five** things you learn about Crescent Bay from these lines.   **[5 marks]**

Read lines 9-15.

A2.   How does the writer show what Crescent Bay looks and sounds like?

You must refer to the text to support your answer, using relevant subject terminology.

    [5 marks]

Read lines 16-28.

A3.   What impressions do you get of the shepherd and the animals from these lines?

You must refer to the language used in the text to support your answer, using relevant subject terminology.   **[10 marks]**

Read lines 29-42.

A4.   How does the writer make these lines vivid and interesting?

You should write about:

- the writer's use of language to make these lines vivid and interesting;
- how the structure of these lines makes them vivid and interesting;
- the effects on the reader.

You must refer to the text to support your answer, using relevant subject terminology.

    [10 marks]

Paper 1 — Questions

Read lines 43 to the end.

A5.   "In the last twenty or so lines of this passage, the writer is successful
       in creating a believable scene and set of characters for the reader."

       To what extent do you agree with this view?

       You should write about:

       • your own impressions of the scene and the characters,
         both here and in the passage as a whole;
       • how the writer has created these impressions.

       You must refer to the text to support your answer.   **[10 marks]**

*Benedict and Eddie thought that the
stick chewing really clinched it for the
believability of their latest roles.*

Section B — Writing

*In this section you will be assessed for the quality of your **creative prose writing** skills.*

*24 marks are awarded for communication and organisation;
16 marks are awarded for vocabulary, sentence structure, spelling and punctuation.*

You should aim to write about 450-600 words.

Choose **one** of the following titles for your writing:

    Either,   *(a)*   Changing Times.

    Or,   *(b)*   The Child on the Empty Street.

    Or,   *(c)*   Write about a time when you were on a school trip.

    Or,   *(d)*   Write a story which begins:
                       I never thought he/she would have been capable of...

                                                       [40 marks]

Paper 1 — Literature Extract

This is the text to go with the questions on pages 62-63. This extract is the opening of a short story set in New Zealand, written in 1922 by Katherine Mansfield.

At the Bay

Very early morning. The sun was not yet risen, and the whole of Crescent Bay was hidden under a white sea-mist. The big bush-covered hills at the back were smothered. You could not see where they ended and the paddocks and bungalows began. The sandy road was gone and the paddocks and bungalows the other side of it; there were no white dunes covered with reddish grass beyond them;

5 there was nothing to mark which was beach and where was the sea. A heavy dew had fallen. The grass was blue. Big drops hung on the bushes and just did not fall; the silvery, fluffy toi-toi* was limp on its long stalks, and all the marigolds and the pinks in the bungalow gardens were bowed to the earth with wetness. Drenched were the cold fuchsias, round pearls of dew lay on the flat nasturtium leaves. It looked as though the sea had beaten up softly in the darkness, as though one immense wave had

10 come rippling, rippling — how far? Perhaps if you had waked up in the middle of the night you might have seen a big fish flicking in at the window and gone again...

Ah-Aah! sounded the sleepy sea. And from the bush there came the sound of little streams flowing, quickly, lightly, slipping between the smooth stones, gushing into ferny basins and out again; and there was the splashing of big drops on large leaves, and something else — what was it? — a faint stirring and

15 shaking, the snapping of a twig and then such silence that it seemed some one was listening.

Round the corner of Crescent Bay, between the piled-up masses of broken rock, a flock of sheep came pattering. They were huddled together, a small, tossing, woolly mass, and their thin, stick-like legs trotted along quickly as if the cold and the quiet had frightened them. Behind them an old sheep-dog, his soaking paws covered with sand, ran along with his nose to the ground, but carelessly,

20 as if thinking of something else. And then in the rocky gateway the shepherd himself appeared. He was a lean, upright old man, in a frieze** coat that was covered with a web of tiny drops, velvet trousers tied under the knee, and a wide-awake*** with a folded blue handkerchief round the brim.

One hand was crammed into his belt, the other grasped a beautifully smooth yellow stick. And as he walked, taking his time, he kept up a very soft light whistling, an airy, far-away fluting that sounded

25 mournful and tender. The old dog cut an ancient caper or two and then drew up sharp, ashamed of his levity, and walked a few dignified paces by his master's side. The sheep ran forward in little pattering rushes; they began to bleat, and ghostly flocks and herds answered them from under the sea. "Baa! Baaa!" For a time they seemed to be always on the same piece of ground.

There ahead was stretched the sandy road with shallow puddles; the same soaking bushes showed

30 on either side and the same shadowy palings****. Then something immense came into view; an enormous shock-haired giant with his arms stretched out. It was the big gum-tree outside Mrs. Stubbs' shop, and as they passed by there was a strong whiff of eucalyptus. And now big spots of light gleamed in the mist. The shepherd stopped whistling; he rubbed his red nose and wet beard on his wet sleeve and, screwing up his eyes, glanced in the direction of the sea. The sun was rising. It was marvellous

35 how quickly the mist thinned, sped away, dissolved from the shallow plain, rolled up from the bush and was gone as if in a hurry to escape; big twists and curls jostled and shouldered each other as the silvery beams broadened. The far-away sky — a bright, pure blue — was reflected in the puddles, and the drops, swimming along the telegraph poles, flashed into points of light. Now the leaping, glittering sea was so bright it made one's eyes ache to look at it. The shepherd drew a pipe, the bowl as small as an

40 acorn, out of his breast pocket, fumbled for a chunk of speckled tobacco, pared off a few shavings and stuffed the bowl. He was a grave, fine-looking old man. As he lit up and the blue smoke wreathed his head, the dog, watching, looked proud of him.

"Baa! Baaa!" The sheep spread out into a fan. They were just clear of the summer colony before the first sleeper turned over and lifted a drowsy head; their cry sounded in the dreams of little

45 children... who lifted their arms to drag down, to cuddle the darling little woolly lambs of sleep. Then

Paper 1, Question A1 — Sample Answer

the first inhabitant appeared; it was the Burnells' cat Florrie, sitting on the gatepost, far too early as usual, looking for their milk-girl. When she saw the old sheep-dog she sprang up quickly, arched her back, drew in her tabby head, and seemed to give a little fastidious shiver. "Ugh! What a coarse, revolting creature!" said Florrie. But the old sheep-dog, not looking up, waggled past, flinging out his
50 legs from side to side. Only one of his ears twitched to prove that he saw, and thought her a silly young female. The breeze of morning lifted in the bush and the smell of leaves and wet black earth mingled with the sharp smell of the sea. Myriads of birds were singing. A goldfinch flew over the shepherd's head and, perching on the tiptop of a spray, it turned to the sun, ruffling its small breast feathers. And now they had passed the fisherman's hut, passed the charred-looking little whare***** where Leila the
55 milk-girl lived with her old Gran. The sheep strayed over a yellow swamp and Wag, the sheep-dog, padded after, rounded them up and headed them for the steeper, narrower rocky pass that led out of Crescent Bay and towards Daylight Cove. "Baa! Baa!" Faint the cry came as they rocked along the fast-drying road. The shepherd put away his pipe, dropping it into his breast-pocket so that the little bowl hung over. And straightway the soft airy whistling began again. Wag ran out along a ledge of
60 rock after something that smelled, and ran back again disgusted. Then pushing, nudging, hurrying, the sheep rounded the bend and the shepherd followed after out of sight.

Glossary
*   tol-tol — a type of tall grass
**   frieze — coarse woollen cloth
***   wide-awake — a type of wide-brimmed hat
**** palings — pointed fence-posts
***** whare — a hut

Now that you're familiar with the text and the questions, the next few pages will help you to look at each of the questions in a bit more detail. There'll be mark schemes and student answers galore. First up is question A1 — it's a simple fact-finding question, so get stuck in and enjoy...

Here's question A1 and a possible answer

Read lines 1-8.

A1.   List **five** things you learn about Crescent Bay from these lines.   **[5 marks]**

1) Question A1 tests your ability to <u>find</u> information or ideas in a <u>specified section</u> of the text. <u>One mark</u> is awarded for each <u>correct</u> piece of information, up to a maximum of <u>five marks</u>.

2) Answers can <u>paraphrase</u> the text or use <u>short quotes</u> — but you should avoid <u>long quotations</u>.

3) Here's an example answer — write how many marks <u>out of 5</u> you think it would get and <u>explain why</u> on the lines below.

A1.	1	*It has hills covered in bushes.*
	2	*There is a sandy road.*
	3	*It is raining in Crescent Bay.*
	4	*There are streams.*
	5	*A heavy dew had fallen.*

This answer gets ☐ mark(s) out of 5 because ....
....
....
....
....

Paper 1, Question A2 — Mark Scheme

This page gives you advice and a mark scheme for marking question A2 of the sample exam.
Read this information and digest it. Then you'll be ready to mark the student answers on p.67.

Here's a reminder of question A2

Read lines 9-15.

A2.   How does the writer show what Crescent Bay looks and sounds like?
You must refer to the text to support your answer, using relevant subject terminology.

[5 marks]

Question A2 is about how the writer creates effects

1) In question A2, answers need to explain how the writer has used <u>language</u> and <u>structure</u> to achieve <u>effects</u>.

2) There are a maximum of <u>five marks</u> available.

3) Points and examples need to come from the <u>correct part</u> of the text (lines 9 to 15).

4) The points all need to be about how the writer describes <u>Crescent Bay</u>.

5) Answers should use the correct <u>technical terms</u> to identify different features of the text.

6) They then need to fully <u>explain</u> the effect that each feature has.

Use this mark scheme for question A2

Here's a table to help you <u>mark</u> the answers on the opposite page. Work out which description <u>fits</u> each sample answer <u>best</u> to find the mark you think it <u>deserves</u>.

Number of marks	What's written	How it's written
5 marks	In-depth and insightful comments about what the bay looks and sounds like. Shows perceptive understanding of how language and structure have been used to achieve effects.	Well-considered, accurate subject terminology used. A wide variety of examples effectively support points throughout.
4 marks	Accurate comments about what the bay looks and sounds like, which show how language and structure have been used to achieve effects.	Subject terminology is used accurately and examples are used effectively to support points.
3 marks	Some explanation of what the bay looks and sounds like, and how language and structure have been used to achieve effects.	Relevant subject terminology used. Relevant examples are used to support points.
2 marks	Simple comments about what the bay looks and sounds like, and some simple identification of the effects of language and structure.	Some relevant subject terminology is used and some examples are used.
1 mark	Some comment on what the bay is like. Little or no mention of language or structural features.	Little to no subject terminology or examples used.

Paper 1, Question A2 — Sample Answers

Now it's your turn to be the examiner.

1) Make sure you've <u>read</u> the <u>advice</u> on page 66.

2) Use it to give the second answer a <u>mark</u> out of 5.
The first answer has already been marked for you.

3) <u>Explain</u> how you've decided on the marks in the lines below the answers.

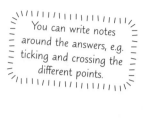
You can write notes around the answers, e.g. ticking and crossing the different points.

Answer 1

A2.   The writer shows there is a lot of water in the bay by describing the sea and the streams. The reader knows that the sea isn't too loud as the writer describes it as "sleepy". The streams sound louder as they are "gushing".
    The writer uses alliteration to describe the sea in the sentence "Ah-Aah! sounded the sleepy sea." The writer also uses onomatopoeia to describe some of the sounds like "splashing".

This answer gets **2** mark(s) out of 5 because *it makes simple comments on what the bay looks and sounds like and uses some subject terminology, but it doesn't go into the effect of the writer's techniques very much. For example, the answer says the writer has used alliteration and onomatopoeia to recreate the sound of the sea and the falling drops of water, but it doesn't explain the effect of these techniques.*

Answer 2

A2.   In this part of the text, the writer focuses on showing what the water in Crescent Bay looks and sounds like. The description goes from the calm tone of the sea to the more energetic tone of the fast-flowing streams, which means the passage builds up in activity, making the "silence" at the end more dramatic.
    The writer uses language to reinforce this build-up. In the first sentence, the writer uses the adverb "softly" to describe the sea, giving the start of the passage a calm tone. The writer then introduces more movement with the repetition of "rippling" when describing the sea. The energetic tone is then added to by the writer's use of several active verbs, for example "flowing" and "slipping".
    The writer also uses sound to help the reader imagine the bay. For example the alliteration of the 's' sound in "sounded the sleepy sea" and "slipping between the smooth stones" is onomatopoeic, which gives the reader a vivid impression of the gentle, dreamlike atmosphere of the bay, and helps them to imagine being surrounded by the soft noises of the scene.

This answer gets [ ] mark(s) out of 5 because ....
....
....
....

Paper 1, Question A3 — Mark Scheme

It's time for question A3. Have a read of this page before marking the answers on page 69.

Here's question A3 again

Read lines 16-28.

A3. What impressions do you get of the shepherd and the animals from these lines?

You must refer to the language used in the text to support your answer, using relevant subject terminology. **[10 marks]**

Question A3 is about how the text affects the reader

1) In question A3, answers need to explain how the writer has used <u>language</u> to achieve <u>effects</u> and <u>influence</u> the reader.

2) There are a maximum of <u>ten marks</u> available.

3) Points and examples need to come from the correct <u>part</u> of the text (lines 16 to 28).

4) The points all need to be about the <u>shepherd and the animals</u> — <u>what</u> impressions of them are created, and <u>how</u> these impressions are created.

5) <u>Technical terms</u> need to be used accurately to identify language features.

6) Answers then need to fully <u>explain</u> the effect that each language feature has, and how the reader is <u>influenced</u>.

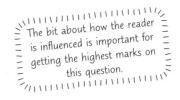
The bit about how the reader is influenced is important for getting the highest marks on this question.

Here's the mark scheme for question A3

1) Look at the table below to work out which set of <u>descriptions</u> fits each answer best. Then award the <u>mark</u> from alongside the descriptions that you think <u>fits best</u>.

2) If the answer <u>clearly</u> does <u>everything</u> in the descriptions, go for the <u>higher mark</u>. If it <u>just about</u> does what the descriptions say, then go for the <u>lower mark</u>.

Number of marks	What's written	How it's written
9-10 marks	In-depth and insightful comments about the shepherd and the animals. Shows perceptive understanding of how language has been used to achieve effects and influence the reader.	Well-considered, accurate subject terminology used. A wide variety of examples effectively support points throughout.
7-8 marks	Accurate comments about the shepherd and the animals, which show how language has been used to achieve effects and influence the reader.	Subject terminology is used accurately and examples are used effectively to support points.
5-6 marks	Some understanding of the impression given of the shepherd and the animals, and how language has been used to achieve effects and influence the reader.	Relevant subject terminology used. Relevant examples are used to support points.
3-4 marks	Simple comments about the shepherd and the animals, and some simple identification of the effects of language.	Some relevant subject terminology is used and some examples are used.
1-2 marks	Some comment on the shepherd and the animals. Little or no mention of language features.	Little to no subject terminology or examples used.

Paper 1, Question A3 — Sample Answers

It's time to be the examiner. Yippee.

1) Make sure you've read the advice and mark scheme on page 68.

2) Use them to give each answer extract a mark out of 10, then explain your reasoning on the dotted lines.

The sample answers here are just extracts. The ones you write in the exam will need to be longer — but you should still mark these out of 10.

Answer 1

A3.   The writer uses adjectives to give the impression that the sheep are vulnerable, for example "small" and "thin". This makes the reader feel sorry for the sheep. The writer says they are a "mass", which also makes them seem vulnerable as it implies they can't survive alone.
    The writer describes the shepherd in lots of detail and also says that he was "taking his time". This shows the reader that he is an experienced shepherd as he isn't worried about the sheep running away.

This answer gets ☐ marks out of 10 because ....
....
....
....
....

Answer 2

A3.   Descriptive verbs such as "huddled" are used to suggest that the sheep are fearful. This is reinforced by the words used to describe their movements: the sheep "trotted along quickly" as if in fear. In contrast, the writer presents the dog as unafraid as it runs along "carelessly". This shows that the dog is a working pet whilst the sheep are animals in captivity.
    The entrance of the shepherd is described using a shorter, less detailed sentence than those that surround it ("And then in the rocky gateway the shepherd himself appeared"). This makes his entrance seem dramatic, which emphasises his authority. This is further shown by his actions: "taking his time", he gently whistles a tune. The effect of this is to show the reader that the shepherd is in total control of what he does.

This answer gets ☐ marks out of 10 because ....
....
....
....
....

Paper 1, Question A4 — Mark Scheme

Question A4 is another 10-mark question. Make sure you're clear on this page before you dive into page 71.

Here's a reminder of question A4

Read lines 29-42.

A4. How does the writer make these lines vivid and interesting?

You should write about:

- the writer's use of language to make these lines vivid and interesting;
- how the structure of these lines makes them vivid and interesting;
- the effects on the reader.

You must refer to the text to support your answer, using relevant subject terminology.

[10 marks]

Question A4 is about the effects of language and structure

1) Question A4 tests the ability to explain how the writer has used <u>language</u>
    and <u>structure</u> to achieve <u>effects</u> and <u>influence</u> the reader.

2) There are a maximum of <u>ten marks</u> available.

3) Points and examples need to come from the <u>correct part</u> of the text (lines 29-42).

4) All the points in the answer need to be about <u>how</u> the writer makes the lines <u>vivid</u> and <u>interesting</u>.

5) Answers should use <u>technical terms</u> and explain the <u>effect</u>
    of each of the language and structure features identified.

This is the mark scheme for question A4

Use the table below to help you mark the answers on the next page. Work out which set of <u>descriptions</u> fits each answer best, then award the <u>mark</u> from alongside the descriptions that you think <u>fits best</u>.

Number of marks	What's written	How it's written
9-10 marks	In-depth and insightful comments about how the lines are made vivid and interesting. Shows perceptive understanding of how language and structure have been used to achieve effects and influence the reader.	Well-considered, accurate subject terminology used. A wide variety of examples effectively support points throughout.
7-8 marks	Accurate comments about how the lines are made vivid and interesting, which show how language and structure have been used to achieve effects and influence the reader.	Subject terminology is used accurately and examples are used effectively to support points.
5-6 marks	Some understanding of how the lines are made vivid and interesting, and how language and structure have been used to achieve effects.	Relevant subject terminology used. Relevant examples are used to support points.
3-4 marks	Simple comments about the lines being vivid and interesting, and some simple identification of the effects of language and structure.	Some relevant subject terminology is used and some examples are used.
1-2 marks	Some comment on what's vivid and interesting about the lines. Little or no mention of language or structural features.	Little to no subject terminology or examples used.

Paper 1, Question A4 — Sample Answers

Here's another pair of answer extracts for you to assess.

1) Make sure you've <u>read</u> the <u>advice</u> and <u>mark scheme</u> on page 70.

2) Use them to give each of these answer extracts a <u>mark</u> out of 10.

3) <u>Explain</u> how you've decided on the marks on the lines below the answers.

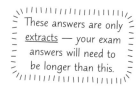
These answers are only <u>extracts</u> — your exam answers will need to be longer than this.

Answer 1

A4.   The writer uses the viewpoint of an omniscient third-person narrator to make these lines vivid and interesting. In this part of the text, the narrator takes the reader on a journey along the "sandy road" with the shepherd, which allows the writer to relate the effect of the mist, gradually revealing the scene. For example, the "shock-haired giant" that the narrator describes becomes a "big gum-tree". This vivid image not only helps the narrator to show what the scene looks like, but also adds interest for the reader on an emotional level: the reader feels the moment of panic and confusion when something unclear appears through the mist.

   The writer then vividly describes the dispersal of the mist using a succession of verbs: the mist "thinned", "dissolved" and "rolled". These verbs are all combined in one long sentence to create the effect of a hurried and confused retreat. This is confirmed by the personification the writer then uses: the mist was "in a hurry to escape". These images help the reader to more clearly imagine the complex and tumultuous sight of the mist rapidly retreating before the rising sun.

This answer gets [   ] marks out of 10 because ....

....

....

....

....

Answer 2

A4.   In this part of the text, the writer describes the sun rising. The writer makes the sunrise sound really beautiful by saying that it is "marvellous", so the lines are vivid and interesting.

   The writer also uses lots of different words to describe the scene before the sun has risen ("sandy road", "soaking bushes" and "big gum-tree") which makes it more vivid in the reader's mind because they can picture it better.

This answer gets [   ] marks out of 10 because ....

....

....

....

....

Paper 1, Question A5 — Mark Scheme

Here's the last question in Section A. It's a bit tricky, so read this page carefully...

Here's question A5 to refresh your memory

Read lines 43 to the end.

A5.   "In the last twenty or so lines of this passage, the writer is successful in creating a believable scene and set of characters for the reader."

To what extent do you agree with this view?

You should write about:

- your own impressions of the scene and the characters, both here and in the passage as a whole;
- how the writer has created these impressions.

You must refer to the text to support your answer.

[10 marks]

Question A5 is about giving your own opinion

1) Question A5 tests the ability to evaluate a text, and to explain your personal opinion on a statement about it. There are a maximum of ten marks available for this question.

2) Your opinion needs to be supported with examples from the text, with an explanation of how each example supports the opinion.

3) Points and examples can come from any part of the text, but should focus on lines 43 to the end.

Use this mark scheme for question A5

Use the table below to help you mark the answers on the next page. Work out which set of descriptions fits each answer best, then award the mark from alongside the descriptions that you think fits best.

Number of marks	What's written	How it's written
9-10 marks	In-depth, personal response to the statement, which shows overview — a clear understanding of how successful the whole text is in creating a believable scene and set of characters. There is a critical, persuasive analysis of how the writer has created effects.	Well-considered, accurate subject terminology used. A wide variety of examples effectively support points throughout.
7-8 marks	A personal response to the statement which shows critical awareness of how successful the text is in creating a believable scene and set of characters. Answer clearly analyses how the writer has created effects.	Subject terminology is used accurately and examples are used effectively to support points.
5-6 marks	An evaluation of the statement which shows some awareness of how successful the text is in creating a believable scene and set of characters. Some analysis of how the writer has created effects.	Relevant subject terminology used. Relevant examples are used to support points.
3-4 marks	A personal opinion on the statement is given which shows limited awareness of how successful the text is in creating a believable scene and set of characters. Limited statements on how the writer has created effects.	Some relevant subject terminology is used and some examples are used.
1-2 marks	A simple personal opinion on the statement is given. Little or no comment on how the writer has created effects.	Little to no subject terminology or examples used.

Paper 1, Question A5 — Sample Answers

Here are two extracts from responses to question A5 for you to mark.

1) Make sure you've <u>read</u> the <u>advice</u> and <u>mark scheme</u> on page 72.

2) Use them to give each of these answer extracts a <u>mark</u> out of 10.

3) <u>Explain</u> how you've decided on the marks on the lines below the answers.

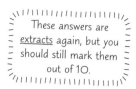

These answers are <u>extracts</u> again, but you should still mark them out of 10.

Answer 1

A5.   I find the text successful in creating believable characters because the writer tells us what they are thinking, for example the cat thinks "'Ugh! What a coarse, revolting creature!'" of the dog. They are believable characters because they are consistent. For example, the dog doesn't care about Florrie and earlier in the text it says he does something "carelessly".

     The scene is also believable because the writer uses sensory language. I think the way the writer describes the smell of the "wet black earth" really helps the reader to imagine what it smells like.

This answer gets [ ] marks out of 10 because ....
....
....
....
....

Answer 2

A5.   In general, I think the writer is successful in creating a believable scene and set of characters, because they use a range of techniques that are effective. I think the scene is made believable because the writer goes beyond visual description into other senses such as smells and sounds, for example "the smell of leaves" and "Myriads of birds were singing". This gives the reader a more complete picture of the scene, so they could imagine being there.

     The writer also tries to involve the reader by giving them insight into what the characters are thinking; for example, the dog trying to ignore Florrie (lines 49-51). This helps to make the characters more believable, as the reader can understand their actions better. The text does this throughout with the dog, but less so with the shepherd or the sheep, so I think that on the whole the dog is more believable than the other characters.

This answer gets [ ] marks out of 10 because ....
....
....
....

Paper 1, Section B — Mark Scheme

This question is worth 40 marks — it's a bit of a whopper. Make sure you know how to mark it.

Here's a quick recap of paper 1, section B

*In this section you will be assessed for the quality of your **creative prose writing** skills.*

24 marks are awarded for communication and organisation;
16 marks are awarded for vocabulary, sentence structure, spelling and punctuation.

You should aim to write about 450-600 words.

Choose **one** of the following titles for your writing:

Either,	(a)	Changing Times.
Or,	(b)	The Child on the Empty Street.
Or,	(c)	Write about a time when you were on a school trip.
Or,	(d)	Write a story which begins: I never thought he/she would have been capable of... **[40 marks]**

Look at this mark scheme for section B

1) Section B tests <u>two</u> things. There are 24 marks for an <u>interesting</u> and <u>well-organised</u> answer, and 16 marks for <u>varied</u> and <u>accurate</u> use of <u>vocabulary</u>, <u>sentence structure</u>, <u>spelling</u> and <u>punctuation</u>.

The texts on the next page are short extracts — so bear in mind that a longer answer would be more fully developed on things like plot.

2) Use the table below to help you mark the answers on the next page. Work out which <u>descriptions</u> fit each answer best, then award the <u>mark</u> from alongside each description that you think <u>fits best</u>.

Communication and organisation		Vocabulary, sentence structure, spelling and punctuation	
20-24 marks	Detailed, imaginative and sophisticated plot and characterisation, which consistently engages the reader's interest. Ambitious use of structure and grammar, so the writing is imaginatively organised, controlled and coherent.	14-16 marks	Confident and ambitious use of a wide range of vocabulary, punctuation and sentence structures. Spelling and punctuation are highly accurate.
15-19 marks	Convincing, detailed plot and characterisation, which engages the reader's interest. Accurate use of structure and grammar, so the writing is well-organised, controlled and coherent.	11-13 marks	A good range of vocabulary, punctuation and sentence structures. Spelling and punctuation are accurate.
10-14 marks	Some detail and development of plot and characterisation, so the reader is often engaged. Writing has structure and uses accurate grammar, so the writing is organised and clear.	7-10 marks	Variation of vocabulary, punctuation and sentence structure. Spelling and punctuation are mostly accurate.
5-9 marks	Some plot and characterisation, without much detail. Starts to show some structure and control of grammar, so the writing has some organisation and clarity.	4-6 marks	Some variation of vocabulary, punctuation and sentence structure. Spelling and punctuation are usually accurate.
1-4 marks	Basic attempt at plot and characterisation. Basic structure and control of grammar, which shows a limited attempt at organisation.	1-3 marks	Limited range of vocabulary, punctuation and sentence structure. Some spelling and punctuation is accurate.

Paper 1, Section B — Sample Answers

Here are two <u>extracts</u> from sample answers to the <u>second</u> title in section B, 'The Child on the Empty Street'.

1) Make sure you've <u>read</u> the <u>mark scheme</u> on page 74.

2) Mark the two criteria <u>separately</u>, then <u>add</u> up both marks to get a total out of 40.

3) <u>Explain</u> how you've decided on the marks on the lines below the answers.

Answer 1

B (b).   The street was empty except for one figure: it was a little boy. He was roughly dressed. His shoelaces were untied or missing. His hair was as messy as a bird's nest. The little boy's T-shirt was lime green with darker green grass stanes.

    He stood out in the street. The houses were organised as neatly as a box of matchsticks. Some of the lawns had flowers — like roses and sunflowers.

    It was a warm, hot evening, just turning dark but with a bit of light. It shone on the boy like an old-fashioned lantern. It lit his face like a torch. There were no clouds and no stars. Just the little boy, alone in the street, all by himself.

Communication and organisation = ☐ / 24

....
....

Vocabulary, sentence structure, spelling and punctuation = ☐ / 16

....
....

Total = ☐ / 40

....
....

Answer 2

B (b).   The sun sets slowly on Oak Street; it clings to the branches of the trees, reluctant to leave. The branches shuffle in its half-light, dappling the pathways below with kaleidoscopic patterns of yellow, orange, black, yellow again. Outside number 42, a cat tries to catch the colours.

    A child walks slowly down oak Street. He pauses to watch the determined tabby playing in the light, stretches out his arm beneath the tree so it, too, is speckled with the rays. The cat is disturbed by the intrusion and, affronted, skulks off to hide.

    The child ambles on. He strokes his fingers through hedges, punts pebbles along the path, tosses acorns into the air. When the trees end he squints in the brightness and shields his eyes as if in a salute. He wonders where the cat is.

Communication and organisation = ☐ / 24

....
....

Vocabulary, sentence structure, spelling and punctuation = ☐ / 16

....
....

Total = ☐ / 40

....
....

Paper 2 — Questions

It's time to be the examiner again. This time, the questions are similar to paper 2 ('19th and 21st Century Non-Fiction Reading and Transactional / Persuasive Writing'). You need to have a look at the sample answers to each of the exam questions, then decide what marks they deserve. Here's a reminder of how to do it:

> 1) Read the sample exam questions and the two texts on pages 76-79.
>
> 2) Remember — you <u>don't</u> have to actually answer the questions.
>
> 3) Instead, on pages 80-89 there are some <u>sample answers</u> for you to <u>mark</u>, with some advice and mark schemes to help you along the way.

Section A — Reading

To answer the following questions you will need to refer to the letter by Charlotte Brontë on page 78.

A1.   (a) Which one of the Sidgwicks does Charlotte Brontë prefer?   **[1 mark]**

       (b) Apart from her sister, who does Charlotte Brontë say is allowed to read the letter?   **[1 mark]**

       (c) Why does Charlotte Brontë stop writing the letter?   **[1 mark]**

A2.   Charlotte Brontë is trying to persuade her sister to feel sympathy for her. How does she try to do this?

     You should comment on:

- what she says to influence her sister's opinion;
- her use of language and tone;
- the way she presents her experiences.   **[10 marks]**

To answer the following questions you will need to refer to the newspaper article by Monica Albelli on page 79.

A3.   (a) Which two groups of people is Monica Albelli referring to when she mentions "two opposing 'teams'"?   **[2 marks]**

       (b) According to the article, what was the name of the oldest child that Monica Albelli looked after?   **[1 mark]**

A4.   What do you think and feel about Monica Albelli's views on being a nanny?

     You should comment on:

- what is said;
- how it is said.

     You must refer to the text to support your comments.   **[10 marks]**

Paper 2 — Questions

To answer the following questions you will need to use both texts.

A5. According to these two writers, why can the relationship between parents and a nanny be difficult?   **[4 marks]**

A6. Both of these texts are about looking after other people's children.

Compare the following:

- the writers' attitudes to looking after other people's children;
- how they get across their points of view.

You must use the text to support your comments and make it clear which text you are referring to.   **[10 marks]**

Why is this hot dog like paper 2 question A6? It uses two sauces...

Section B — Writing

*Answer Question B1 **and** Question B2.*

For each question, 12 marks are awarded for communication and organisation; 8 marks are awarded for vocabulary, sentence structure, punctuation and spelling.

Think about the purpose and audience for your writing.

You should aim to write about 300-400 words for each task.

B1. The government is proposing to make volunteering with young children compulsory for all 16- to 18-year-olds, to help prepare them for the challenges of raising a family.

You have been asked to give a speech to your local council to share your views on this proposal. You could argue in favour or against this proposal.

Write a lively speech for your local council giving your views.   **[20 marks]**

B2. Your school is keen to make sure all students are eating a healthy diet.

Write a report for the school governors suggesting ways this might be done.

You could include:

- examples of the ways in which students aren't currently eating healthily;
- your ideas about how the situation could be improved.

[20 marks]

Paper 2 — 19th-Century Source

The following text was written by Charlotte Brontë, a famous 19th-century author. Charlotte was working as a governess — a woman employed to teach and care for the children in a household. This is an extract from a letter written to her sister in 1839.

Dearest Lavinia,*

I am most exceedingly obliged to you for the trouble you have taken in seeking up my things and sending them all right. The box and its contents were most acceptable.

I have striven hard to be pleased with my new situation. The country, the house, and the
5   grounds are, as I have said, divine. But, alack-a-day! there is such a thing as seeing all beautiful around you — pleasant woods, winding white paths, green lawns, and blue sunshiny sky — and not having a free moment or a free thought left to enjoy them in. The children are constantly with me, and more riotous, perverse, unmanageable cubs never grew. As for correcting them, I soon quickly found that was entirely out of the question: they are to do as they like. A complaint to Mrs. Sidgwick
10   brings only black looks upon oneself, and unjust, partial excuses to screen the children. I have tried that plan once. It succeeded so notably that I shall try it no more. I said in my last letter that Mrs. Sidgwick did not know me. I now begin to find that she does not intend to know me, that she cares nothing in the world about me except to contrive how the greatest possible quantity of labour may be squeezed out of me, and to that end she overwhelms me with oceans of needlework, yards of cambric
15   to hem, muslin night-caps to make, and, above all things, dolls to dress. I do not think she likes me at all, because I can't help being shy in such an entirely novel scene, surrounded as I have hitherto been by strange and constantly changing faces. I see now more clearly than I have ever done before that a private governess has no existence, is not considered as a living and rational being except as connected with the wearisome duties she has to fulfil. While she is teaching the children, working for
20   them, amusing them, it is all right. If she steals a moment for herself she is a nuisance. Nevertheless, Mrs. Sidgwick is universally considered an amiable woman. Her manners are fussily affable. She talks a great deal, but as it seems to me not much to the purpose. Perhaps I may like her better after a while. At present I have no call to her. Mr. Sidgwick is in my opinion a hundred times better — less profession, less bustling condescension, but a far kinder heart.
25   As to Mrs. Collins' report that Mrs. Sidgwick intended to keep me permanently, I do not think that such was ever her design. Moreover, I would not stay without some alterations. For instance, this burden of sewing would have to be removed. It is too bad for anything. I never in my whole life had my time so fully taken up.

Don't show this letter to papa or aunt, only to Branwell.** They will think I am never satisfied
30   wherever I am. I complain to you because it is a relief, and really I have had some unexpected mortifications to put up with. However, things may mend, but Mrs. Sidgwick expects me to do things that I cannot do — to love her children and be entirely devoted to them. I am really very well. I am so sleepy that I can write no more. I must leave off. Love to all. — Good-bye.

C. BRONTË.

Glossary
*   A nickname for Charlotte's sister, Emily.
**   Branwell — their brother.

Paper 2 — 21st-Century Source

The following text is an extract from an article written by a nanny, Monica Albelli.
It was published in a broadsheet newspaper in 2013.

Confessions of a Nanny

Being a nanny — whether you're a Mary Poppins, a Nanny McPhee or a Mrs Doubtfire — is
a very tricky job. You have to be liked by two opposing "teams" to which a "perfect" nanny means
completely different things. "You must be kind, you must be witty, very sweet and fairly pretty...
If you don't scold and dominate us, we will never give you cause to hate us" — this is how the
5 children in Mary Poppins, Michael and Jane, want the newspaper ad for their nanny to read. Their
father, Mr Banks, is keener on discipline. Mrs Banks seems to believe perfection lies somewhere in
between that and the children's ideal.

I have always loved children and had a natural ability to connect with them with ease, no
matter their gender, nationality or character. But when you're a nanny, kids come with parents.
10 And parents come with problems, opinions and expectations of their own, often in conflict between
themselves.

Lesley, a successful publisher, and Brian, a dentist, were Scots in their mid-40s. They
worked long hours but seemed to love Therese, seven, Tom, nine, and William, 11. Their approach
when it came to the kids' upbringing though was completely different from each other. Confident
15 and motivated, Lesley believed her children's time should be spent doing homework, reading
books or playing educational games. Brian, cheerful and laid back, wanted us to "just have fun".
He asked me not to be strict with the kids, while Lesley kept pressuring me to turn them into
responsible and hard-working individuals. I would arrive at their house to find a note from Brian,
asking me to take them to the park, and then receive a text from Lesley with a to-do list.
20 Lesley would often come home late to find the kids already asleep. "I'm not a good mum,"
she once confessed. "I'm actually a bit jealous. I think they are starting to like you more than they
like me."

I reassured her that this was not true and that she was doing her best.

The kids and I had bonded. Once, as I was getting ready to leave, Tom curled around my
25 leg, while Lesley tried to persuade him he had to let me go. They liked having me around so much
that they started asking Brian if I could sleep over. Had we bonded too much?

Then things changed. Lesley seemed upset about something, and Brian was more and more
absent. One day they told me they wouldn't be needing me any more as they had decided to get
an au pair, who could also help with the house. I knew that wasn't the real reason. They had, I
30 realised, been asking me to become everything they weren't and, as soon as I started to achieve
that, they felt threatened.

I tried to see it from their point of view. Being a nanny is difficult, but being a parent is even
harder. Having a nanny is also hard.

I remembered what a friend used to say whenever I shared my frustrations with her: "You
35 care too much. It's just a job."

Should a nanny be indifferent, see herself as a doctor and treat all family members as her
patients, being impartial and never getting emotionally involved? How can Mary Poppins be
indifferent? She is cool and funny, strict at times, but always caring — the perfect nanny. But she is
a fictional character, and so are Mr and Mrs Banks, and Michael and Jane.
40 Many dysfunctional families later, I have learned to care at the same time as keeping a
distance, and that there is no such thing as the perfect family — or the perfect nanny.

Paper 2, Questions A1 and A2

And now for some answers... student answers, mind. These pages will help with questions A1 and A2.

Here's question A1 and its answers

A1. (a) Which one of the Sidgwicks does Charlotte Brontë prefer? **[1 mark]**

(b) Apart from her sister, who does Charlotte Brontë say is allowed to read the letter? **[1 mark]**

(c) Why does Charlotte Brontë stop writing the letter? **[1 mark]**

Question A1 tests your ability to <u>find</u> information or ideas. Here's an example answer — write how many marks <u>out of 3</u> you think it would get and <u>explain why</u> on the lines below.

A1. (a) Mr Sidgwick
(b) Her father
(c) Because she is sleepy.

This answer gets ☐ mark(s) out of 3 because ....
....
....
....

Use the information below to mark question A2

A2. Charlotte Brontë is trying to persuade her sister to feel sympathy for her. How does she try to do this?

You should comment on:

- what she says to influence her sister's opinion;
- her use of language and tone;
- the way she presents her experiences. **[10 marks]**

Look at the table below to work out which set of <u>descriptions</u> fits each answer best. Then award the <u>mark</u> from alongside the descriptions that you think <u>fits best</u>.

The answers to be marked are on the opposite page.

Number of marks	What's written	How it's written
9-10 marks	In-depth and insightful comments about how Brontë persuades her sister. Shows perceptive understanding of how language and structure have been used to achieve effects and influence the reader.	Well-considered, accurate subject terminology used. A wide variety of examples effectively support points throughout.
7-8 marks	Accurate comments about how Brontë persuades her sister, which show how language and structure have been used to achieve effects and influence the reader.	Subject terminology is used accurately and examples are used effectively to support points.
5-6 marks	Some understanding of how Brontë persuades her sister, and how language and structure have been used to achieve effects and influence the reader.	Relevant subject terminology used. Relevant examples are used to support points.
3-4 marks	Simple comments about how Brontë persuades her sister, and some simple identification of the effects of language and structure.	Some relevant subject terminology is used and some examples are used.
1-2 marks	Some comment on Brontë being persuasive. Little or no mention of language features.	Little to no subject terminology or examples used.

Paper 2, Question A2 — Sample Answers

Here are two extracts from responses to question A2 for you to try marking.

1) Make sure you've <u>read</u> the <u>advice</u> and <u>mark scheme</u> on page 80.

2) Mark the <u>second</u> answer — the <u>first</u> answer has already been marked.

3) <u>Explain</u> how you've decided on the marks on the lines below the answers.

The sample answers here are just extracts. The ones you write in the exam will need to be longer — but you should still mark these out of 10.

Answer 1

A2.   Charlotte Brontë uses a metaphor: she says that Mrs Sidgwick gives her "oceans of needlework". She is comparing the jobs she is given to an ocean, which would help her sister understand that they're enormous.

    Charlotte's work seems very overwhelming. She tells her sister that she has "no existence" apart from her "duties", and "can't help being shy". This descriptive language makes it seem like her job has taken over her life, so her sister might have felt sympathy for her when she read that.

This answer gets | 4 | marks out of 10 because *the answer begins to look at how Charlotte Brontë has written in a persuasive way to her sister. There are some comments on the effects of language on the reader, although the analysis isn't very in-depth. Some technical terms are used, but "descriptive language" isn't used accurately. The answer uses some suitable quotes, but "can't help being shy" is irrelevant.*

Answer 2

A2.   Brontë uses a combination of formal and informal language in order to influence her sister. She uses polite, formal language in places, such as the phrase "I am most exceedingly obliged"; this is a courtesy that would make her sister feel pleased. This formal language is then combined with familiar terms like "papa" and informal phrases, such as "Love to all" to appeal to the relationship between Brontë and her sister, which has the overall effect of making Brontë more likeable. This in turn would make her sister more inclined to agree with Brontë's viewpoint.

    Brontë's language is also used to express her viewpoint in a strong and compelling way, which helps to influence her sister into sympathising with her difficulties. For example, she uses a list of adjectives, describing the children she takes care of as "riotous, perverse, unmanageable". The cumulative effect of these negative adjectives helps to emphasise Brontë's displeasure with her current situation, which encourages her sister to sympathise with her difficulties.

This answer gets | | marks out of 10 because ....
....
....
....
....

Paper 2, Questions A3 and A4

It's time for questions A3 and A4. Get stuck in, and before you know it, it'll be time for question A5...

Here's question A3 and its answers

A3. (a) Which two groups of people is Monica Albelli referring to when she mentions "two opposing 'teams'"? **[2 marks]**

(b) According to the article, what was the name of the oldest child that Monica Albelli looked after? **[1 mark]**

Question A3 is similar to question A1 — it tests your ability to <u>find</u> information or ideas. Here's an example answer — write how many marks <u>out of 3</u> you think it would get and <u>explain why</u> on the lines below.

A3. (a) *Children and their nannies.*

(b) *William*

This answer gets [ ] mark(s) out of 3 because ....
....
....
....

Question A4 is about evaluating the text

A4. What do you think and feel about Monica Albelli's views on being a nanny?

You should comment on:

- what is said;
- how it is said.

You must refer to the text to support your comments. **[10 marks]**

Question A4 tests the ability to <u>evaluate</u> texts by giving a <u>personal response</u>. Look at the table below to work out which set of <u>descriptions</u> fits each answer best — then award the <u>mark</u> that you think <u>fits best</u>.

Number of marks	What's written	How it's written
9-10 marks	In-depth, personal evaluation of the text, which shows overview — a clear understanding of how successful the whole text is at conveying Albelli's views on being a nanny. There is a critical, persuasive analysis of how the writer has created effects.	Well-considered, accurate subject terminology used. A wide variety of examples effectively support points throughout.
7-8 marks	A personal evaluation of the text, which shows critical awareness of how successful the text is at conveying Albelli's views on being a nanny. Answer clearly analyses how the writer has created effects.	Subject terminology is used accurately and examples are used effectively to support points.
5-6 marks	An evaluation of the text which shows some awareness of how successful the text is at conveying Albelli's views on being a nanny. Some analysis of how the writer has created effects.	Relevant subject terminology used. Relevant examples are used to support points.
3-4 marks	A personal opinion on the text is given, which shows limited awareness of how successful the text is at conveying Albelli's views on being a nanny. Limited statements on how the writer has created effects.	Some relevant subject terminology is used and some examples are used.
1-2 marks	A simple personal opinion on the text is given. Little or no comment on how the writer has created effects.	Little to no subject terminology or examples used.

Paper 2, Question A4 — Sample Answers

Pens at the ready — it's time to have a go at marking some more answer extracts.

1) Make sure you've read the advice and mark scheme on page 82.
2) Use them to give each of these answer extracts a mark out of 10.
3) Explain how you've decided on the marks on the lines below the answers.

These answers are only extracts — your exam answers will need to be longer than this.

Answer 1

A4.   Monica Albelli makes me feel sympathetic towards her and the views she has on being a nanny. She makes me feel sympathetic from the first sentence when she says being a nanny "is a very tricky job". She then uses an interesting example (Mary Poppins), which helps me to understand her points better.
    She uses a detailed example of a family that she worked for, which illustrates her view: that it's hard to be a nanny and that a nanny should care but keep a distance. The example shows how she learnt this, so I feel more sympathetic to her opinion of how a nanny should behave.

This answer gets [ ] marks out of 10 because ....

....

....

....

....

Answer 2

A4.   Monica Albelli is trying to show the reader that she thinks being a nanny is difficult, and she does this in a convincing way. At the beginning she gives three examples of famous fictional nannies, then she talks about her own experience and how she found working with the parents to be "difficult". The idea of the fictional nannies helps her to show that in real life, being a "perfect" nanny like them is impossible.
    One of the ways that Albelli shows how being a nanny is difficult is the list of nouns she uses in the second paragraph. She says that parents have "problems, opinions and expectations" and that there is also "conflict" between parents as well. Having two sets of all these things to cope with would be very difficult, so the reader is made to agree with the writer.

This answer gets [ ] marks out of 10 because ....

....

....

....

....

Paper 2, Question A5 — Mark Scheme

Question A5 is a tricky one, so read the information on this page carefully.

Here's a reminder of question A5

A5. According to these two writers, why can the relationship between parents and a nanny be difficult?

[4 marks]

Question A5 is about combining information from both texts

1) Question A5 tests the ability to pick out <u>information</u> from <u>both texts</u> about why the relationship between parents and a nanny can be difficult, then write a <u>summary</u>.

2) A summary is a piece of writing that <u>combines</u> the ideas from both texts, but is more <u>concise</u> and is written in your <u>own words</u>.

3) There are a maximum of <u>four marks</u> available — so there shouldn't be any <u>unnecessary detail</u>.

4) Answers don't need to <u>compare</u> the two texts — they just need to <u>summarise</u> what the texts <u>say</u> about why the relationship between parents and a nanny can be difficult.

5) <u>Evidence</u> from <u>both texts</u> should be included to back up the points that are being made.

Mark Ranger, Mark Jones, Mark Smith and Mark Forsyth were all delighted to be given to the GCSE student.

Use this mark scheme for question A5

Here's a table to help you <u>mark</u> the answers on the opposite page. Work out which description <u>fits</u> each sample answer <u>best</u> to find the mark you think it <u>deserves</u>.

Number of marks	What's written
4 marks	Answer combines information from both texts, showing a clear understanding of why the relationship between parents and a nanny can be difficult. Answer provides an overview, based on a range of examples that are used effectively to support points throughout.
3 marks	Answer combines information from both texts, showing some understanding of why the relationship between parents and a nanny can be difficult. Answer uses examples from both texts to support points.
2 marks	Answer identifies a range of relevant information from both texts. Relevant examples are used to support points.
1 mark	Answer selects some relevant details from both texts.

Paper 2, Question A5 — Sample Answers

Here's a pair of answers for you to assess.

1) Make sure you've read the advice and mark scheme on page 84.
2) Use them to give each of these answers a mark out of 4.
3) Explain how you've decided on the marks on the lines below the answers.

Answer 1

A5.   Charlotte Brontë shows that the relationship between parents and a nanny can be difficult because of discipline: the woman Brontë works for doesn't want her "correcting" the children, and she thinks she should.

Monica Albelli talks about how the people she worked for didn't agree about how the children should spend their time, and that must have made her frustrated with them both as it made it difficult for her to do her job well.

Also, it is hard because the nanny might be unsure whether she should love the children or not: it might "upset" the parents, as Monica Albelli found out.

This answer gets [ ] marks out of 4 because ....

....

....

....

Answer 2

A5.   Both texts show that the relationship between parents and a nanny can be difficult as conflict can arise between their viewpoints. In the case of Charlotte Brontë, her attempt at "correcting" the children brought "black looks" upon her: it is made clear that Mrs Sidgwick has a different approach to Brontë, and thinks badly of her as a result. Monica Albelli, meanwhile, found herself in a position where she was being pressured to be "strict" by one parent and told to "just have fun" by the other. This made it extremely difficult for her to please both her employers.

The question of how much a nanny should do in their role can also make their relationship with parents difficult. Brontë is extremely unhappy with the amount of "wearisome duties" she is given by Mrs Sidgwick and she doesn't like her as a result: she says she has "no call to her". Albelli, though, had "bonded too much" with the children in her care, going too far with her duties and ultimately upsetting her employers. Both issues result in problems for the nanny: Albelli was ultimately dismissed and Brontë is unwilling to stay in her position permanently.

This answer gets [ ] marks out of 4 because ....

....

....

....

Paper 2, Question A6 — Mark Scheme

Question A6 is the last question in section A, and it's about comparing the two texts.

Have a read of question A6 to refresh your memory

A6. Both of these texts are about looking after other people's children.

Compare the following:
- the writers' attitudes to looking after other people's children;
- how they get across their points of view.

You must use the text to support your comments and make it clear which text you are referring to. **[10 marks]**

Question A6 is about comparing the writers' attitudes

1) Question A6 tests the ability to compare <u>how</u> the writers express their <u>viewpoints</u>.

2) There are a maximum of <u>ten marks</u> available for this question.

3) Answers need to <u>identify</u> the writers' viewpoints, <u>support</u> these observations with <u>examples</u> from the text, and then explain <u>how</u> these examples convey the writers' points of view.

4) Answers also need to fully <u>develop</u> each point by making <u>links</u> between the texts and <u>comparing</u> the attitudes of <u>both</u> writers.

Use this mark scheme to assess question A6

Use the table below to help you mark the answers on the next page. Work out which set of <u>descriptions</u> fits each answer best, then award the <u>mark</u> from alongside the descriptions that you think <u>fits best</u>.

Number of marks	What's written	How it's written
9-10 marks	A detailed, insightful comparison of the writers' attitudes, which demonstrates a perceptive understanding of the differences and / or similarities between the two viewpoints. In-depth analysis of the methods each writer uses to convey their point of view.	Well-considered, accurate subject terminology used. A wide variety of examples effectively support points throughout.
7-8 marks	The writers' attitudes are clearly compared, showing a detailed understanding of the differences and / or similarities between the two viewpoints. Answer includes relevant discussion of the methods used to convey both writers' ideas.	Subject terminology is used accurately and examples are used effectively to support points.
5-6 marks	Some attempt to compare writers' attitudes, identifying some differences and / or similarities between their viewpoints and commenting on techniques used to convey them.	Relevant subject terminology used. Relevant examples are used to support points.
3-4 marks	Identification of the two writers' main attitudes and basic description of the differences and / or similarities between them. Makes a few very simple references to methods used.	Some relevant subject terminology is used and some examples are used.
1-2 marks	Identification of basic differences and / or similarities between the writers' attitudes.	Little to no subject terminology or examples used.

Paper 2, Question A6 — Sample Answers

Here are two <u>extracts</u> from student responses to question A6 for you.

1) Make sure you've <u>read</u> the <u>advice</u> and <u>mark scheme</u> on page 86.
2) Use them to give each of these student answers a <u>mark</u> out of 10.
3) <u>Explain</u> how you've decided on the marks on the lines below the answers.

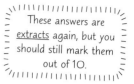
These answers are <u>extracts</u> again, but you should still mark them out of 10.

Answer 1

A6.　　　Brontë's letter suggests that she feels limited and confined by the duties involved in looking after other people's children. She refers to her wards as being "constantly" with her. Brontë's choice of adverb suggests that she gets no respite from the children; it also indicates that she resents this constant imposition, and does not think it's fair that she's expected to be so involved in the children's lives.

　　　Albelli indicates a similarly close proximity to her wards: the image of the young boy "curled" around her leg is a symbol of the closeness between them. However, she uses rhetorical questions to suggest that this closeness is desirable, which challenges negative attitudes such as Brontë's. She questions "How can Mary Poppins be indifferent?", to suggest that nannies should aim to be close to children in their care, even whilst maintaining some degree of professional detachment.

This answer gets ☐ marks out of 10 because ....
....
....
....
....

Answer 2

A6.　　　Both writers think that looking after children is hard — Brontë describes her job as a "burden", which suggests that it's hard. Monica Albelli calls being a nanny "tricky" and "difficult". However, the two writers are different about why they think it's hard. Brontë doesn't like being asked to "love" somebody else's children and she says she "cannot" do it. Albelli finds it hard not to bond "too much" with her children.

　　　The writers are also different because Albelli likes looking after other people's children, but Brontë doesn't. She says it's "riotous". Albelli's friend says "You care too much", showing that Albelli does care about her work.

This answer gets ☐ marks out of 10 because ....
....
....
....
....

Paper 2, Questions B1 and B2 — Mark Scheme

To B1 or to B2, that is the question... and the answer is both, and they're both 20-mark beasties.

Here are questions B1 and B2 again

B1. The government is proposing to make volunteering with young children compulsory for all 16- to 18-year-olds, to help prepare them for the challenges of raising a family.

You have been asked to give a speech to your local council to share your views on this proposal. You could argue in favour or against this proposal.

Write a lively speech for your local council giving your views. [20 marks]

B2. Your school is keen to make sure all students are eating a healthy diet.

Write a report for the school governors suggesting ways this might be done.

You could include:

- examples of the ways in which students aren't currently eating healthily;
- your ideas about how the situation could be improved. [20 marks]

Here's the mark scheme for questions B1 and B2

1) For both B1 and B2, there are 12 marks for writing interesting content that is well-organised, and 8 marks for varied and accurate use of vocabulary, sentence structure, spelling and punctuation.

2) Use the table below to help you mark the answers on the next page. Work out which descriptions fit each answer best, then award the mark from alongside each description that you think fits best.

Communication and organisation		Vocabulary, sentence structure, spelling and punctuation	
11-12 marks	Writing is imaginatively and consistently matched to form, purpose and audience, with a confidently adapted register. Content is sophisticated and ambitious, including lots of relevant detail. Structure is elaborate and engaging.	8 marks	Confident and ambitious use of a wide range of vocabulary, punctuation and sentence structures. Spelling and punctuation are highly accurate.
8-10 marks	Writing is consistently matched to form, purpose and audience, with a sustained, well-adapted register. Content is detailed and well thought-out, and includes relevant subject matter. Structure is organised and clear.	6-7 marks	A good range of vocabulary, punctuation and sentence structures. Spelling and punctuation are accurate.
5-7 marks	Writing is matched to form, purpose and audience, with an appropriately adapted register. Content has some detail, and includes some relevant subject matter. Writing is structured.	4-5 marks	Variation of vocabulary, punctuation and sentence structure. Spelling and punctuation are mostly accurate.
3-4 marks	Writing has been partly matched to form, purpose and audience, and there has been some attempt to adapt the register. Content is limited in detail, and there has been some attempt at structure.	2-3 marks	Some variation of vocabulary, punctuation and sentence structure. Spelling and punctuation are usually accurate.
1-2 marks	Basic attempt at matching writing to form, purpose and audience, and basic adaptation of register. Simple content, with a simple attempt at structure.	1 mark	Limited range of vocabulary, punctuation and sentence structure. Some spelling and punctuation is accurate.

Paper 2, Questions B1 and B2 — Sample Answers

Here's one extract from a sample answer to question B1 and one from a sample answer to question B2.

1) Make sure you've read the advice and mark scheme on page 88.
2) Mark each of the criteria separately, then add up the marks to get a total out of 20.
3) Explain how you've decided on the marks on the lines below the answers.

These are just extracts, but you should still give them a mark out of 20.

Answer 1

B1.　　In a nutshell, the idea of a Young People's Volunteer Programme is a deeply flawed concept. Whilst volunteering with children is undoubtedly an effective way for young people to experience the trials of parenthood, the Programme has a number of practical and logistical difficulties, which shed serious doubt on its advisability.

　　Young people simply do not have time to volunteer. They are already ground to the bone, juggling home life and academics in the hope of getting that important first job. Moreover, the assumption that all young people will one day have children is outdated; up to 10% of young people say that they do not wish to become a parent. Thirdly, and perhaps most importantly, humans have raised children since time began. Why waste time when we are evolutionarily primed to be good parents?

Communication and organisation = ☐ / 12 ....

Vocabulary, sentence structure, spelling and punctuation = ☐ / 8 ....

Total = ☐ / 20 ....

Answer 2

B2.　　This report is written for the school governors to suggest ways that they can make sure all students eat a more healthy diet. First, students don't like to be told what they can and can't eat, so the school shouldn't just tell them what to do. The problem is that students like to eat burgers, chips and sausages, so whenever they're available then they'll buy them. Therefor you should make the canteen always put some healthy food on the same plate as the unhealthy food, like putting a salad with a burger, so they get a bit of both to start with.

　　Second, loads of students don't eat breakfast, so then they eat unhealthy snacks at break times. Therefor it would be a good idea to write to parents to suggest they make sure their kids eat breakfast.

Communication and organisation = ☐ / 12 ....

Vocabulary, sentence structure, spelling and punctuation = ☐ / 8 ....

Total = ☐ / 20 ....

Paper 1 — Questions

This section has two <u>practice exam papers</u> in it. They're similar in style to the two exams you'll take for your WJEC Eduqas GCSE in English Language.

To start with, try this practice exam for <u>paper 1</u>. Try to answer these questions as if you were in a real exam — give yourself <u>1 hour 45 minutes</u> to read the literature extract and answer <u>all</u> the questions.

Section A — Reading

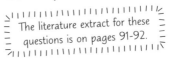
The literature extract for these questions is on pages 91-92.

---

*In this section, you should spend about **10 minutes** reading the passage and all the questions. Then you should spend about **50 minutes** answering **all 5 questions**.*

Read lines 1-8.

A1.   List **five** things from this part of the text about the child.   **[5 marks]**

Read lines 12-23.

A2.   How does the writer describe the child's trip to buy the ice cream?

You must refer to the language used in the text to support your answer, using relevant subject terminology.   **[5 marks]**

Read lines 24-34.

A3.   What impressions do you get of the child's family from these lines?

You must refer to the text to support your answer, using relevant subject terminology.

[10 marks]

Read lines 35-44.

A4.   How does the writer create a sense of calm and monotony in these lines?

You should write about:

- the way the characters' actions create a sense of calm and monotony;
- the writer's use of language to build up a sense of calm and monotony;
- the effects on the reader.

You must refer to the text to support your answer, using relevant subject terminology.

[10 marks]

Now consider the passage as a whole.

A5.   "The writer is successful in making this passage tense."

To what extent do you agree with this view?

You should write about:

- your own impressions of the tension in the passage as a whole;
- how the writer has created these impressions.

You must refer to the text to support your answer.   **[10 marks]**

Paper 1 — Literature Extract

Section B — Writing

*In this section you will be assessed for the quality of your **creative prose writing** skills.*
*You should spend about **10 minutes** planning and about **35 minutes** writing.*

24 marks are awarded for communication and organisation.
16 marks are awarded for vocabulary, sentence structure, spelling and punctuation.

You should aim to write about 450-600 words.

Choose **one** of the following titles for your writing:

Either,	*(a)*	The Journey.
Or,	*(b)*	The Misty Morning.
Or,	*(c)*	Write about a time when you went for a walk.
Or,	*(d)*	Write a story which begins: After all these years, who would have thought that... **[40 marks]**

Paper 1 — Literature Extract

This is the text to go with the questions on page 90. It's the opening of a short story by Ray Bradbury, written in 1946. The story, set in 1927, is about a young boy living in a small town in the USA.

The Night

You are a child in a small town. You are, to be exact, eight years old, and it is growing late at night. Late for you, accustomed to bedding in at nine or nine-thirty: once in a while perhaps begging Mom or Dad to let you stay up later to hear Sam and Henry on that strange radio that is popular in this year of 1927. But most of the time you are in bed and snug at this time of night.

5 It is a warm summer evening. You live in a small house on a small street in the outer part of town where there are few street lights. There is only one store open, about a block away: Mrs Singer's. In the hot evening Mother has been ironing the Monday wash and you have been intermittently begging for ice cream and staring into the dark.

You and your mother are all alone at home in the warm darkness of summer. Finally, just before it is time for
10 Mrs Singer to close her store, Mother relents and tells you:

'Run get a pint of ice cream and be sure she packs it tight.'

You ask if you can get a scoop of chocolate ice cream on top, because you don't like vanilla, and Mother agrees. You clutch the money and run barefooted over the warm evening cement sidewalk, under the apple trees and oak trees, toward the store. The town is so quiet and far off, you can only hear the crickets sounding in the
15 spaces beyond the hot indigo trees that hold back the stars.

Your bare feet slap the pavement, you cross the street and find Mrs Singer moving ponderously about her store, singing Yiddish* melodies.

'Pint ice cream?' she says. 'Chocolate on top? Yes!'

You watch her fumble the metal top off the ice-cream freezer and manipulate the scoop, packing the
20 cardboard pint chock full with 'chocolate on top, yes!' You give the money, receive the chill, icy pack, and rubbing it across your brow and cheek, laughing, you thump barefootedly homeward. Behind you, the lights of the lonely little store blink out and there is only a street light shimmering on the corner, and the whole city seems to be going to sleep ...

Opening the screen door you find Mom still ironing. She looks hot and irritated, but she smiles just the same.
25 'When will Dad be home from lodge-meeting?' you ask.

'About eleven-thirty or twelve,' Mother replies. She takes the ice cream to the kitchen, divides it. Giving you

Paper 1 — Literature Extract

your special portion of chocolate, she dishes out some for herself and the rest is put away. 'For Skipper and your father when they come.'

Skipper is your brother. He is your older brother. He's twelve and healthy, red-faced, hawk-nosed,
30 tawny-haired, broad-shouldered for his years, and always running. He is allowed to stay up later than you. Not much later, but enough to make him feel it is worthwhile having been born first. He is over on the other side of town this evening to a game of kick-the-can and will be home soon. He and the kids have been yelling, kicking, running for hours, having fun. Soon he will come clomping in, smelling of sweat and green grass on his knees where he fell, and smelling very much in all ways like Skipper; which is natural.

35 You sit enjoying the ice cream. You are at the core of the deep quiet summer night. Your mother and yourself and the night all around this small house on this small street. You lick each spoon of ice cream thoroughly before digging for another, and Mom puts her ironing board away and the hot iron in its case, and she sits in the armchair by the phonograph**, eating her dessert and saying, 'My lands, it was a hot day today. It's still hot. Earth soaks up all the heat and lets it out at night. It'll be soggy sleeping.'

40 You both sit there listening to the summer silence. The dark is pressed down by every window and door, there is no sound because the radio needs a new battery, and you have played all the Knickerbocker Quartet records and Al Jolson and Two Black Crows records*** to exhaustion: so you just sit on the hardwood floor by the door and look out into the dark dark dark, pressing your nose against the screen until the flesh of its tip is molded into small dark squares.

45 'I wonder where your brother is?' Mother says after a while. Her spoon scrapes on the dish. 'He should be home by now. It's almost nine-thirty.'

'He'll be here,' you say, knowing very well that he will be.

You follow Mom out to wash the dishes. Each sound, each rattle of spoon or dish is amplified in the baked evening. Silently, you go to the living room, remove the couch cushions and, together, yank it open and
50 extend it down into the double bed that it secretly is. Mother makes the bed, punching pillows neatly to flump them up for your head. Then, as you are unbuttoning your shirt, she says:

'Wait awhile, Doug.'

'Why?'

'Because. I say so.'

55 'You look funny, Mom.'

Mom sits down a moment, then stands up, goes to the door, and calls. You listen to her calling and calling Skipper. Skipper, Skiiiiiiiiiperrrrrrrr over and over. Her calling goes out into the summer warm dark and never comes back. The echoes pay no attention.

Skipper, Skipper, Skipper.

60 *Skipper!*

And as you sit on the floor a coldness that is not ice cream and not winter, and not part of summer's heat, goes through you. You notice Mom's eyes sliding, blinking; the way she stands undecided and is nervous. All of these things.

She opens the screen door. Stepping out into the night she walks down the steps and down the front
65 sidewalk under the lilac bush. You listen to her moving feet.

She calls again. Silence.

She calls twice more. You sit in the room. Any moment now Skipper will reply, from down the long long narrow street:

'All right, Mom! All right, Mother! Hey!'

70 But he doesn't answer. And for two minutes you sit looking at the made-up bed, the silent radio, the silent phonograph, at the chandelier with its crystal bobbins gleaming quietly, at the rug with the scarlet and purple curlicues**** on it. You stub your toe on the bed purposely to see if it hurts. It does.

Whining, the screen door opens, and Mother says:

'Come on, Shorts. We'll take a walk.'

Glossary
* Yiddish — a language spoken by some Jewish people
** phonograph — an old-fashioned device used for playing music records (sometimes called a gramophone)
*** Knickerbocker Quartet, Al Jolson and Two Black Crows — famous entertainment acts in the 1920s
**** curlicues — decorative curls or twists

Paper 2 — Questions

This practice exam is similar in style to <u>paper 2</u> (the non-fiction paper) of your WJEC Eduqas GCSE in English Language.

To make the most of this practice paper, read the texts and do the questions as if you were in the exam, giving yourself <u>2 hours</u> to complete the lot.

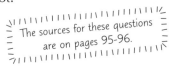
The sources for these questions are on pages 95-96.

Section A — Reading

*Answer **all** of the following questions.*

*In this section, you should spend about **10 minutes** reading the sources and all the questions. Then you should spend about **50 minutes** answering **all 6 questions**.*

To answer the following questions you will need to refer to the newspaper article by Jenni Russell on page 95.

A1.   (a)   Where did Jo and Genevieve first meet each other?   **[1 mark]**

         (b)   What time did Genevieve ring to cancel the film?   **[1 mark]**

         (c)   According to the text, how old might some people be before they become grandparents?   **[1 mark]**

A2.   Jenni Russell is trying to persuade us that friends are important. How does she try to do this?

         You should comment on:

- what she says to influence readers;
- her use of language and tone;
- the way she presents her argument.   **[10 marks]**

To answer the following questions you will need to refer to the extract by Wilkie Collins on page 96.

A3.   (a)   Why does the beggar think he can't find work?   **[1 mark]**

         (b)   Why will Wilkie Collins only collect money from his publisher's at night?   **[1 mark]**

         (c)   What is the name of Wilkie Collins's servant?   **[1 mark]**

A4.   What do you think and feel about Wilkie Collins's views on his Boisterous Friend?

         You should comment on:

- what is said;
- how it is said.

You must refer to the text to support your comments.   **[10 marks]**

Paper 2 — Questions

To answer the following questions you will need to use both texts.

A5.   According to these two writers, why can relationships with other people be problematic?   **[4 marks]**

A6.   Both of these texts are about friendship. Compare the following:

- the writers' attitudes to friendship;
- how they get across their views.

You must use the text to support your comments and make it clear which text you are referring to.   **[10 marks]**

Section B — Writing

*Answer Question B1 **and** Question B2.*

*In this section you will be assessed for the quality of your writing skills. You should spend **30 minutes** on each question — about **5 minutes** planning, and about **25 minutes** writing.*

For each question, 12 marks are awarded for communication and organisation; 8 marks are awarded for vocabulary, sentence structure, punctuation and spelling.

Think about the purpose and audience for your writing.

You should aim to write about 300-400 words for each task.

B1.   Your headteacher is keen to ensure that new students at your school are able to settle in and make friends.

Write a letter to the headteacher suggesting ways this could be done.

You could include:

- examples of the difficulties that new students encounter;
- your ideas about things that could be done to help new students.   **[20 marks]**

B2.   A proposal has been made to make studying one foreign language compulsory up until the age of 18.

You have been asked to write an article about the proposal from a student's perspective, to be published in a broadsheet newspaper. You could write in favour or against this proposal.

Write a lively article for the newspaper giving your views.   **[20 marks]**

Paper 2 — 21st-Century Source

The following text is an extract from an article in a broadsheet newspaper
by a journalist called Jenni Russell. It was published in 2005.

What are friends for?

Earlier this year, I rang my friend Jo and found her in a state of stunned misery.

Jo is a witty, sexy, single, childless woman in her 40s. She's a talented artist, but earns very
little. Without a career, money, husband or family to bolster her confidence, a small group of friends
have been a key part of her identity. Genevieve, an ambitious, glamorous woman whom she met at
5 university, has been her constant confidante* for almost a quarter of a century. But in the past three
or four years, Genevieve has become increasingly unreliable: making dates she later cancels; slow to
return calls or emails.

Last winter, Jo arranged for them to go to a film together, only for Genevieve to ring at 6pm to say
she was awfully sorry, but she had to spend the evening with some dreary Burmese** refugees, friends
10 of her father's. Fortunately for Jo, 20 minutes later she was rung and asked to make up the numbers
for a formal dinner party. When she walked into the room, she felt as if she had been punched in the
stomach. Genevieve was sitting on the sofa, flirting with the men on either side of her. There were no
refugees.

"The next day I sent her an email saying: 'Why did you lie to me? Why not just say: I want to go to
15 a dinner party? I can take that. I can't take being lied to. This is a friendship. We're supposed to trust
one another.' She emailed back immediately saying she didn't have to explain herself to me. And then
a month later she said our friendship had run its course, and she wouldn't be seeing me any more. It's
one of the worst things that's ever happened to me. And I haven't just lost her; I've lost all our history,
all that shared experience."

20 Often, we don't know where we fit into friends' lives. Are we in the first dozen, or the remotest 90
in their circle? If they ask us to dinner once a year, is that an honour because they only entertain twice,
or a sign of our unimportance, because they hold dinners every week?

This degree of uncertainty exists partly because many of us now lead lives in which we are the only
connecting thread. It is perfectly possible for much of our lives to be opaque to anyone who knows us.
25 They may only ever encounter one particular facet of our existence, because we can, if we choose, keep
parents, past acquaintances, old partners, colleagues, friends, and neighbours in totally separate boxes.
Many people value the anonymity and freedom that gives them. The flip side is that just as we are not
known, so we cannot really know others.

Talking to a wide range of people, it was clear that few of them are really happy with the friendships
30 they have. People with consuming jobs are sad that they haven't had the time to build stronger bonds,
and wonder whether it's too late to develop them; mothers with time to spare want to find new friends
but don't know how. Many people would like to have more friends, or deeper, warmer, more reliable
relationships than the ones they have now, but don't know how to go about it.

There are powerful reasons why we should create these bonds, even if we only start when we are
35 older. The phenomenon of later births means families take up a smaller percentage of our lives. We
wait years to have children, and we could be 70 before we become grandparents for the first time. We
have more time available, and fewer familial responsibilities, than the generations before us. We all
want to feel needed and valued by others. It is possible for friends to fill that need, but only if we work
at it.

40 It isn't easy, because friendship is a subtle dance, and no one wants to be explicitly pursued
when it's unwelcome, or explicitly dropped when they are not wanted. Nor does it come with any
guarantees. People are unpredictable. But we need to play the game of friendship. Evidence shows
that people with close friends live longer and are happier than those without. And friendship defines
what it means to be human.

Glossary
*   confidante — a close friend; someone you talk to about private matters
**   Burmese — from a country in Southeast Asia that's currently known as Burma or Myanmar

Paper 2 — 19th-Century Source

This is an extract from a piece by Wilkie Collins, which appeared in a periodical called 'Household Words' in 1858. A periodical was a collection of fiction and non-fiction that related to the topics of the day, published once a week or once a month (similar to a modern magazine). Collins has just described a beggar addressing a crowd in the street — this extract starts with his report of the beggar's speech.

Save me from my friends

"Good Christian people, will you be so obliging as to leave off your various occupations for a few minutes only, and listen to the harrowing statement of a father of a family, who is reduced to acknowledge his misfortunes in the public streets? Work, honest work, is all I ask for; and I cannot get it. Good Christian people, I think it is because I have no friends. Must I perish in a land of plenty because I have

5 no work and because I have no friends?"

"No friends!" I repeated to myself, as I walked away. But can the marvellous assertion be true? Can this enviable man really go home and touch up his speech for to-morrow, with the certainty of not being interrupted? I am going home to finish an article, without knowing whether I shall have a clear five minutes to myself, all the time I am at work. Can he take his money back to his drawer, in broad daylight,

10 and meet nobody by the way who will say to him, 'Remember our old friendship, and lend me a trifle'? I have money waiting for me at my publisher's, and I dare not go to fetch it, except under cover of the night. No wonder that he looks prosperous and healthy, though he lives in a dingy slum, and that I look peevish and pale, though I reside on gravel, in an airy neighbourhood.

It is a dreadful thing to say (even anonymously); but it is the sad truth that I could positively dispense

15 with a great many of my dearest friends.

There is my Boisterous Friend, for instance. I always know when he calls, though my study is at the top of the house. I hear him in the passage, the moment the door is opened. I have told my servant to say that I am engaged, which means simply, that I am hard at work. "Dear old boy!" I hear my Boisterous Friend exclaim, with a genial roar, "writing away, the jolly, hard-working, clever old chap, just as usual —

20 eh, Susan? Lord bless you! he knows me — he knows I don't want to interrupt him." My door is burst open, as if with a battering-ram (no boisterous man ever knocks), and my friend rushes in like a mad bull. "Ha, ha, ha! I've caught you," says the associate of my childhood. "Don't stop for me, dear old boy; I'm not going to interrupt you (Lord bless my soul, what a lot of writing!) — and you're all right, eh? No! I won't sit down; I won't stop another instant. So glad to have seen you dear fellow — good bye." By this

25 time, his affectionate voice has made the room ring again; he has squeezed my hand, in his brotherly way, till my fingers are too sore to hold the pen; and he has put to flight, for the rest of the day, every idea that I had when I sat down to work. Could I really dispense with him? I don't deny that he has known me from the time when I was in short frocks*, and that he loves me like a brother. Nevertheless, I could dispense — yes, I could dispense — oh, yes, I could dispense — with my Boisterous Friend.

30 I have not by any means done yet with the number of my dear friends whom I could dispense with. To say nothing of my friend who borrows money of me (an obvious nuisance), there is my self-satisfied friend, who can talk of nothing but himself, and his successes in life; there is my inattentive friend, who is perpetually asking me irrelevant questions, and who has no power of listening to my answers; there is my hospitable friend, who is continually telling me that he wants so much to ask me to dinner, and who never

35 does really ask me by any chance.

A double knock at the street door stops my pen suddenly. A well-known voice in the passage smites my ear, inquiring for me, on very particular business, and asking the servant to take in the name. This is my friend who does not at all like the state of my health. Well, well, I have made my confession, and eased my mind. Show him in, Susan — show him in.

Glossary
* short frocks — the short dresses that very young children (both male and female) often wore

Answers

Section One — Exam Basics

Page 1: Planning Answers

1. a) lines 12-21
   b) Uncle William
2. Here are some things you could mention:
   - The plan uses clear stages to explain a point of view.
   - Includes arguments and counter-arguments.
   - All points are relevant to the question.
   - Gives examples to help illustrate points.
   - Conclusion gives an opinion on the report.
   - Conclusion clearly summarises the argument.
   - Conclusion answers the question.
3. E.g. Para 1: Pets are a huge responsibility — risk that pupils might neglect them.
   Para 2: Unfair on parents, who will be forced to help students out.
   Para 3: Would also strain school budgets (give statistics).
   Conclusion: Should look for other ways to teach students responsibility.

Pages 2-3: P.E.E.D.

1. a) and c) should be ticked
2. a) Example: e.g. "you can become a real-life tomb explorer"
      Explanation: e.g. makes the reader feel like they can get involved with the experience.
   b) Example: "explore, quest and hunt"
      Explanation: e.g. makes the experience seem continuously action-filled.
3. a) Any sensible answer, e.g. "determined".
   b) Any example that is relevant to the answer in a), e.g. "she was going to do it her way and it'd be all the better for it"
   c) Answers need to explain the example in b), e.g. "This quote links two firm statements in a compound sentence, which suggests that Alice is feeling confident and decisive."
   d) Answers should develop the answer in c), e.g. "Alice's determination to plan her own trip may also suggest that she'll have some interesting experiences, which draws the reader into the story."

Pages 4-5: Writing Well

1. a) Overall, the writer in Source A demonstrates a more positive attitude towards breeding cats.
   b) The writer in Source B doesn't include other people's point of view, so they're very biased.
   c) The writer in Source B tries to convince the reader using an anecdote about cat breeding.
2. a) E.g. The metaphor "a furious battleground" suggests that the house is very chaotic.
   b) E.g. The conversation between Sam and Nina tells you how the characters are feeling.
3. reinforce; Furthermore; emphasises; signifying
4. Another point of view is, Secondly, In addition to this, Conversely
5. Paragraph breaks should be inserted as below. Phrases in bold can be replaced by any other sensible linking phrase.

   The extract from the biography argues that Orson Welles' career was a "magnificent failure". It points to the fact that his greatest achievement, 'Citizen Kane', was made before the age of thirty.

   In contrast, the magazine article argues that Orson Welles was a wonderful director and actor throughout his career. It suggests that people like the "myth" of Orson Welles' fall from grace and ignore his later achievements.

   Finally, the third text, the interview with Orson Welles, shows that he himself had conflicting feelings towards his career and achievements. The interviewer describes him as "fiercely proud" of his films, but also "insecure beneath the bravado".

Pages 6-7: Reading with Insight

1. a) The character is looking forward to something.
   b) The character is feeling exhausted.
   c) The character is feeling uncomfortable.
2. Words and phrases which imply the writer dislikes Hitchcock's later films could include:
   - "leaden in their pace and tone"
   - "increasingly dull"
   - "self-conscious style of film"
   Words and phrases which imply the writer likes Hitchcock's early films could include:
   - "still delight"
   - "wonderful humour"
   - "lightness of touch"
   - "masterpieces"
   Words and phrases which imply the writer dislikes Hitchcock as a person could include:
   - "gorged himself"
   - "substantial ego"
3. Example: e.g. "cheated"
   Explanation: e.g. "The writer uses this word to emphasise how they feel they've been misled by the restaurant owner, which is intended to make the restaurant owner feel guilty."
4. Answers must be backed up with relevant evidence, e.g. Ed is feeling nervous in this passage, which is suggested by his body language: the writer says he "shifted his weight from one foot to the other" and "He took a deep breath". This sense of nervousness is reinforced using the passage's dialogue: the woman says that Ed looks "a bit peaky".

Pages 8-9: Spelling, Punctuation and Grammar

1. a) I jumped out of the taxi, narrowly missing a very large puddle by the kerb.
   b) Keeley said she wanted a tablet, a pair of shoes and some more make-up.
   c) As the boat glided past, its bright paint glinting in the sun, I was able to see the captain saluting me, his gold braid fluttering in the breeze.
2. Answers that should be ticked:
   unnatural, disappear, immediately, occasional
   Answers that should be corrected:
   arguement — argument
   neccessarily — necessarily
   favorite — favourite
   embarassed — embarrassed
   concsious — conscious
   decieved — deceived
   figarative — figurative
   consience — conscience
3. a) I didn't want to go; the leaden sky threatened rain.
   b) Have you ever wondered what it would be like to travel in time? It'd be fantastic!
   c) You can come to my party as long as you bring an expensive present, lovingly wrapped; stay until the end, which will be 2 am; clear up any spillages; and serve the drinks.
4. a) E.g. There <u>was</u> no reason to <u>have</u> a fire drill during the exam.
   b) E.g. Hannah should <u>have</u> eaten the sandwich before <u>its</u> expiry date.

Answers

5.   As he stepped out of the exam hall on that <u>T</u>uesday morning, Rashid breathed an enormous sigh of relief. He wouldn't need to do <u>any</u> more practice papers, and his days of revision and stress were finished. He could <u>have</u> shouted with joy. It was over, and <u>hopefully</u> it had been worth it. He felt the scientific equations <u>evaporate</u> from his mind like morning dew. As Rashid leant gently against the wall to steady himself, he was overcome by the <u>knowledge</u> that his life was now his. He <u>wasn't</u> sure exactly what it would bring, but that was part of the excitement<u>.</u>

Section Two — Reading: Understanding Texts

Pages 10-11: Finding Information and Ideas

1. b) Dani is nervous about going on the roller coaster.
2.   Last weekend we found ourselves with nothing to do on a warm, sunny day, so we decided on a trip to the zoo. The entrance to the zoo was via a <u>rusty</u> iron gate that looked <u>in serious need of repair</u>. We went into the ticket office, only to discover that <u>the floor was filthy</u>; as we looked closer, we realised <u>there was revolting leftover food scattered everywhere</u>. Inside, the animals looked <u>malnourished and miserable</u> in their enclosures, which all seemed <u>dull and empty</u>, with <u>precious little space</u> for them to run around. All in all, <u>a pretty depressing place</u>.
3. Any three correct facts about the garden, either paraphrased or a brief direct quote. Answers need to be from the correct part of the text. For example:
   - There is a bench in the garden.
   - The bench takes up most of the space in the garden.
   - The garden is "tiny".
   - There is a fence in the garden.
   - The fence has gaps in it.
   - There is grass in the garden.
   - The grass is damp.
   - There is an apple tree in the garden.
   - The apple tree is in the corner of the garden.
4. Any five correct facts about George, either paraphrased or a brief direct quote. For example:
   - George has a nasal voice.
   - George has a loud voice.
   - George is wearing a "garish purple suit".
   - George has an "elaborate hairstyle".
   - George brings a bottle of wine to the party.
   - George has "greasy" hands.
   - George is wearing several rings.
   - George likes whisky.
5. a) a fortnight   b) to stay out of the rain   c) archery

Pages 12-13: Summarising Information and Ideas

1. Meat-eaters: Eating meat is natural for human beings and provides nutrients that are important for human health.
   Vegetarians: Eating meat is unnatural for human beings and can cause health problems.
2. E.g.
   Reason: It makes people happier.
   Evidence from 19th-century text: The writer says that playing an instrument will "incite" happiness in their son's "soul".
   Evidence from 21st-century text: The writer says there is evidence to show that people who play a musical instrument have "higher levels" of happiness.

3. Answers should use relevant quotes or examples from both texts to clearly answer the question. Here are some things you could mention:
   - People should read because it can entertain for long periods of time. The 19th-century writer says that they can read for "hours and hours", and the 21st-century text says that you can read for "hours on end".
   - People should read because it is educational. The 19th-century writer says that they have learnt about "fascinating places" from books, and the 21st-century writer says that books have widened their "horizons".
4. Answers should use relevant quotes or examples from both texts to clearly answer the question. Here are some things you could mention:
   - The writers say that people should visit Huntingham Castle because it is beautiful: the writer of the 19th-century diary mentions the "fine grounds and gardens", and the 21st-century review describes the gardens as "divine" and the river as "picturesque".
   - Both writers mention the portrait gallery as a reason to visit the castle: the writer of the 19th-century diary calls it "impressive" and the writer of the 21st-century review describes it as "incredible".

Pages 14-15: Audience and Purpose

1. a) adults   b) novices
2. a) To advise   b) To entertain   c) To persuade
3. E.g.
   Word or phrase: "earn a few quid"
   Explanation: Uses slang in order to relate to the reader.
   Word or phrase: "find us on social media."
   Explanation: Refers to something used regularly by young people to suggest that the company is modern and fun.
4. All your points should use relevant examples and terminology, and comment on the effects of the language used. Here are some things you could mention:
   - Use of puns / wordplay to make the attraction seem fun, e.g. "you'll have a whale of a time", "shaken by a shark", which attracts young people's attention in particular.
   - Uses the phrase "special underwater world" to appeal to a younger audience's sense of adventure.
   - Mentions school and school holidays ("we're open every day in the school holidays") to show that they cater to young people's needs.
5. All your points should use relevant examples and terminology, and comment on the effects of the language used. Here are some things you could mention:
   - Rhetorical questions ("We've all been there, haven't we?") create a sense of familiarity with the reader. This makes them more likely to agree with the writer's opinions.
   - Hyperbole ("sudden and deathly terror") and a simile ("like headless chickens") persuade the reader by making it seem ridiculous to feel stressed about Christmas.
   - Use of direct address ("Britain, we need to take a stand") to create an authoritative tone, which persuades the reader by making the writer seem very confident in their opinions.

Pages 16-17: Informative and Entertaining Texts

1. a) I   b) E   c) I
2. E.g. The first sentence ("The woman was incredibly old.") is short and direct, creating a sense of drama that engages the reader. The phrase "clink and clank" is onomatopoeic, which appeals to the reader's senses to help them imagine the scene.
3. a) Two of the following:
   - There are eight thermal pools.
   - Each pool is a different temperature.
   - The temperature of the hottest pool is 40 degrees.

Answers

b) E.g. The writer describes the hottest pool as "immersive", helping the reader to imagine it as an intense experience.

4. Your answer should offer an opinion on the statement. It should comment on the techniques the writer uses to make the text entertaining and to present the character, using relevant examples and terminology to support each point. Here are some things you could mention:
   - Humorous images such as having to be "surgically removed from her game console" are entertaining for the reader, and show Jasmine's addictive personality.
   - The use of hyperbole to establish that Jasmine has a humorously over-dramatic personality — "more daunting than an icy trek over an Arctic precipice".
   - Narrative viewpoint allows the reader an insight into Jasmine's thoughts, e.g. "Those girls terrified her", which suggests that she may be shy — this hint at another side to her personality adds interest for the reader.

5. All your points should use relevant examples and terminology, and comment on the effects of the language used. Here are some things you could mention:
   - The inclusion of informative dates and facts — "The Battle of Hastings was fought on October 14th 1066".
   - Statements such as "it was the Normans' most important victory over the Anglo-Saxons", which are used to convey information in a clear, direct way.
   - The use of a simile ("trampled like insects") to make the text more entertaining to read.
   - The use of descriptive verbs such as "stormed" and "ambushed" to create a sense of action and excitement, increasing the entertainment value for the reader.

Pages 18-19: Texts that Argue, Persuade or Advise

1. a) To argue   b) To advise   c) To persuade
2.

Technique	Example from text
rhetorical question	"Should such beauty go unsupported?"
opinion stated as fact	"Flamingos are the most fascinating birds in the world." OR "Their beguiling beauty is unrivalled in the animal kingdom."
expert opinion	"Flamingos really are wonderful animals." OR "A dedicated breeding programme would be invaluable to their endurance as a species."
direct address to the reader	"you can help fund the establishment of breeding programmes"

3. Example: e.g. "you could consider"
   Explanation: e.g. It reassures the reader that the text is giving helpful suggestions, not authoritative commands.

4. All your points should use relevant examples and terminology, and comment on the effects of the language used. Here are some things you could mention:
   - Casual style to make the reader comfortable, e.g. "Unless you've been living under a rock for the past month".
   - Use of the imperative form ("don't panic", "have a look") to give clear guidance to the reader.
   - Introductory/concluding paragraphs create a clear structure and summarise the information to make it easier for the reader to understand.

5. All your points should use relevant examples and terminology, and comment on the effects of the language used. Here are some things you could mention:
   - Strong descriptive vocabulary such as "horrified", "dangerous" and "fatal" to convey the idea that Swampy Water is a bad product.

- Lists all of the arguments in one paragraph, linked by words like "Firstly", "Secondly" and "Finally" to give the impression that there are lots of good arguments in the writer's favour.
- Presents the opinion of the writer as fact ("clearly idiotic", "any sane parent would endorse") to make the reader think that the writer's opinion is valid.

Pages 20-21: Writer's Viewpoint and Attitude

1. a) negative   b) positive   c) balanced
2. a) iii)   b) iv)   c) ii)   d) i)
3. Answers need to use examples from both texts to summarise a similarity and a difference between their views, e.g.
   The writers agree that mobile phones should be banned from lessons. Source A says that they are a "nightmare" for teachers, and the writer in Source B is "not about to suggest" they should be allowed in lessons either.
   The writers disagree that mobile phones should be banned from school entirely. The first writer says it's the "best way" to prevent the disruptions, but the second writer believes there's no "harm" in them being used at lunchtimes.
4. Answers should clearly compare the different ideas and techniques in each text, using quotations to support points. Here are some things you could mention:
   - In the 19th-century letter, the writer illustrates their dislike of a new art style using hyperbole ("nothing short of an abomination"). In the 21st-century newspaper article, the writer expresses their admiration for a new art style, also using hyperbole ("They're revolutionaries").
   - Both texts use formal language, e.g. "I read with concern" in the 19th-century letter, "progression in the medium" in the 21st-century newspaper article. This makes their opinion seem more important / authoritative.
   - The 21st-century writer makes the restrictions of traditional art seem negative using a metaphor, "the iron shackles of 'traditional art'", whereas the writer of the 19th-century letter thinks that the rules of traditional art are good: new artists should have "learnt from" older examples.
5. Answers should clearly compare the different ideas and techniques in each text, using quotations to support points. Here are some things you could mention:
   - The texts use figurative language to convey their emotions about rail transport. The 19th-century diary uses a simile to make the steam train seem new and exciting: "shiny as a new penny", whilst the 21st-century speech uses a metaphor to compare the passing trains to a "non-stop army", which makes them seem relentless and invasive.
   - The 21st-century speech is trying to persuade the audience, so it uses rhetorical devices such as repetition ("like me") and direct address ("Residents of Station Crescent!") in an attempt to engage them. The 19th-century text is a diary, so it doesn't contain any overtly persuasive language. It's more descriptive, e.g. "curled into the summer sky".

Pages 22-23: Literature and Literary Non-Fiction

1. a) 3   b) 1   c) 2
2. a) As I stared at the letter, no longer absorbing the words on the page, I realised <u>my hands were starting to shake</u>. <u>How dare they!</u> After all I'd done for that family... their betrayal <u>cut me like a knife</u>. Without even realising it, I'd begun to <u>tear the paper into pieces; ripping, shredding, mutilating</u> the letter until I was left with a pile of limp paper-snowflakes. Then, just for good measure, I aimed <u>a sharp kick</u> at the pile, scattering it across the carpet.
   b) Answers should explain how one of the underlined phrases above creates an impression of the narrator's anger. E.g.
   The writer uses an exclamation, "How dare they!", to emphasise the writer's sense of injustice.

Answers

3. fact; biographies; purpose; argument; entertain; dialogue
4. Your answer should comment on the techniques used to present the characters, using relevant examples and terminology. Here are some things you could mention:
    *   Dialogue gives an insight into each character's mindset, such as Annie: "Don't be ridiculous." and Lucas: "They'll kill me." This encourages the reader to think that Annie is calmer and less dramatic in comparison to Lucas.
    *   The cumulative use of short sentences in Lucas's speech emphasises his stress to the reader, e.g. "I've looked everywhere. It's lost. They'll kill me."
    *   The contrast between the two characters makes each character's personality stand out more and gives the sense that their personalities are two extremes. E.g. the adjectives used to describe Lucas's actions ("frantic", "manic") contrast with the adverbs used to describe Annie, who acts "cautiously" and "calmly".
5. Answers should clearly compare the different ideas and techniques in each text, using quotations to support points. Here are some things you could mention:
    *   The two sources use very different tones to convey their attitudes. The 19th-century speech has an emphatic tone — the speaker repeats the word "must", which emphasises the inflexibility of his beliefs. The 21st-century text is less direct: it conveys its viewpoint using anecdotal evidence.
    *   The 19th-century speech uses an analogy to convey the idea that teaching should be very strict and disciplined — he compares the "schoolmaster" to a "military officer" and pupils to "troops", which suggests that he believes schools should be run as strictly as armies.
    *   The 21st-century writer also believes discipline is important — from the "indistinct" memories of the writer's past, it is the memory of his strict teacher that stands out the most: it is still "clear as day" to him. This simile indicates that Mr Wan was the most important thing about the writer's time at school.

Pages 24-25: 19th-Century Texts

1. a) Catherine is Sir Edward's niece.
    b) The Spears family, because Albert Withers was ill.
    c) "an agreeable gathering" or "much happiness felt by all involved"
2. a) E.g. The writer thinks that social class is very important, and that people from different social classes shouldn't mix.
    b) E.g. The writer thinks that sending children away to boarding school is necessary, but she finds it emotionally difficult.
3. Your answer should evaluate the text by giving an opinion on it. It should comment on the techniques the writer has used to convey her views on her daughter's behaviour, using relevant examples and terminology to support each point. Here are some things you could mention:
    *   The reader is shown that the writer strongly disapproves of her daughter's behaviour through the use of powerful negative adjectives such as "ghastly" and "dangerous".
    *   Phrases such as "your doting and loving mother" suggest that the writer loves her daughter, encouraging the reader to think that her disapproval is partly motivated by concern for her daughter's welfare.
    *   The references to "social standing" and "reputation" might also make the reader think that the writer is trying to avoid a potential scandal caused by her daughter's behaviour.

4. Your answer should evaluate the text by giving an opinion on it. It should comment on the techniques the writer has used to convey their views on educating children, using relevant examples and terminology to support each point. Here are some things you could mention:
    *   The speaker uses emotive phrases such as "poor Tommy" to convey his view that children with no education deserve compassion. This language invokes the audience's emotions, leading them to feel sympathy for the children.
    *   The speaker clearly shows that education is important because of the wider effects that it can have. They link a lack of education to "poverty" and "crime", which makes the audience think about its wider impact.
    *   The phrase "we condemn them" suggests that the speaker thinks he and his audience are responsible for the lack of education for poor children. This might make the audience feel it is their duty to help improve the situation.

Section Three — Reading: Language and Structure

Pages 26-27: Tone, Style and Register

1. a) angry b) detached c) upbeat d) sentimental
2. a) "Customers are advised that we do not accept credit cards."
    b) "It is essential to ensure you have the correct tools before proceeding."
    c) "If you have financial complications, contact our trained advisors."
3. Evidence might include:
    *   Slang is used, e.g. "cheesed off".
    *   Humour is used, e.g. "River C and Swamp D".
    *   Contractions are used, e.g. "It's".
4. All your points should use relevant examples and terminology, and comment on the effects of the language, tone and style used. Here are some things you could mention:
    *   Personification (the sun was "shining triumphantly"), suggesting that even inanimate objects reflect Konrad's positive attitude, creating an upbeat tone.
    *   A simile — the puddles "glittered like molten silver" — which takes something that is usually negative and presents it in a positive, beautiful way.
    *   The idea that everything "promised summer" and the phrase "for whom anything was possible," which create a sense of hope and optimism about the future.
5. All your points should use relevant examples and terminology, and comment on the effects of the language, tone and style used. Here are some things you could mention:
    *   Colloquial phrases like "up to your neck" and "bag loads of new skills" create an informal style, which encourages a young audience to connect with the writer.
    *   The inclusion of the sentence "There's nothing wrong with wanting a break." shows that the writer understands the mindset of young people.
    *   The last two sentences on the page are short and punchy, which creates a tone of excitement that appeals to a young audience.

Pages 28-29: Words and Phrases

1.

Adjectives	Adverbs
threatening	boastfully
lovely	tragically
phenomenal	bitterly
contemptuous	devotedly

2. E.g. "sneered" suggests that Angus doesn't really want to congratulate Madge.

Answers

3.	E.g. "whispered" suggests that the speaker and listener are working together, whilst "spat" suggests that the speaker doesn't like the listener.
4.	E.g. The phrase "I am sure" creates a confident tone that makes the reader more likely to agree with the author. The writer also refers to the reader as "my dear friend" to suggest familiarity, encouraging the reader to listen to the writer.
5.	All your points should use relevant examples and terminology, and comment on the effects of the words and phrases used. Here are some things you could mention:
	•	The repetition of the word 'wind' — "a bitter wind, a stinging wind, a wind that drowned..." — to emphasise the overwhelming nature of the wind.
	•	Words and phrases that indicate noise: "roaring cacophony", "howling", "roar", to appeal to the reader's senses and make the storm more vivid.
	•	Violent verbs, such as "barged", "wrenched" and "savaged", to emphasise that the storm is destructive.
6.	All your points should use relevant examples and terminology, and comment on the effects of the words and phrases used. Here are some things you could mention:
	•	Words and phrases associated with cold to emphasise the woman's detached personality ("icily", "stone cold").
	•	The phrases "breath caught painfully" and "sweat prickling like needles" suggest that the man's fear is physically painful.
	•	The simile "like a condemned man", which emphasises that the man feels resigned to his fate, and indicates that the woman is in a position of great power.

Pages 30-31: Metaphors, Similes and Analogy

1.	a) M b) M c) S d) M
2.	compares; images; non-fiction; persuade
3.	E.g. The second text compares the water to something that the reader is familiar with, to make it easier to visualise.
4.	E.g. The writer is trying to create the impression that the night sky is something precious and beautiful.
5.	All your points should use relevant examples and terminology, and comment on the effects of the analogy used. Here are some things you could mention:
	•	The similarities between the Ferrari and the human body are emphasised, using mechanical terms like "fuel" and "systems" to refer to aspects of taking care of yourself. This persuades the reader that you should take as much care of the human body as you would a Ferrari.
	•	The writer emphasises the differences between a sports car and a human body to support their point further — they suggest that unlike a sports car, a human body is "priceless" and that you can't just "trade this engine in" for a new one, which persuades the reader that they should take even greater care of it.
6.	All your points should use relevant examples and terminology, and comment on the effects of the metaphors and similes used. Here are some things you could mention:
	•	The use of a metaphor to make the environment seem hard and unforgiving — "The landscape was dull steel."
	•	The use of animal similes and metaphors to indicate how vulnerable the workers are — "like mice in a cage", "lambs" — in contrast to the soldiers, who are "wolves".
	•	The use of a simile to suggest the officer in charge of the prisoners has a forceful, unfriendly personality — "fired his orders like cannon balls."

Pages 32-33: Personification, Alliteration and Onomatopoeia

1. a)	personification. E.g. Makes the computer seem like it's mocking the writer, which conveys the writer's frustration.

b)	onomatopoeia. E.g. Helps the reader to imagine the noise created by the students.
c)	alliteration. E.g. Makes the text more memorable.
2.	E.g.
	Personification: "a challenging foe"
	Effect of personification: makes the walk seem rewarding, by suggesting that the walkers have to fight something to complete it.
	Alliteration: "Wilderness Walk"
	Effect of alliteration: makes the name of the walk more memorable, so that readers remember to sign up for it.
3.	All your points should use relevant examples and terminology, and comment on the effects of the onomatopoeia and personification used. Here are some things you could mention:
	•	Onomatopoeia such as "cracking" and "shrill screech" interrupt the tense silence of the forest, creating moments of drama.
	•	Personification of the forest as a living being to create a sense of danger: "purposefully trying to deceive and confuse them."
	•	The personification of the shadows as "delighted", which contrasts with the generally menacing / unhappy tone of the extract, making them seem sinister and teasing. This might make the reader feel afraid or vulnerable.
4.	All your points should use relevant examples and terminology, and comment on the effects of the alliteration, onomatopoeia and personification used. Here are some things you could mention:
	•	The alliterative phrase "twist and turn", which uses a repeated 't' sound to draw the reader's attention to and emphasise the complexity of the streets in Kuala Lumpur.
	•	Personification of the side streets, which wind around "like snakes". This helps the reader to visualise how confusing the streets are by comparing them to something alive and unpredictable.
	•	Onomatopoeic verbs such as "whine" and "buzz" help to create a vivid scene for the reader by recreating the irritating, persistent sounds of the "thousands of scooters".

Pages 34-35: Irony and Sarcasm

1.	opposite; intended; context; humour; offence; cruel
2.	The second extract should be ticked.
	Examples should highlight the contradiction between the positive phrases, e.g. "Ivan is a brilliant secretary", and the negative context, e.g. "he keeps forgetting to bring a pen".
3.	E.g. The writer uses irony to suggest that the characters have a light-hearted attitude to the conversation. For example, Maya uses irony to joke about her job: "It's a trial, that's for sure."
4.	All your points should use relevant examples and terminology, and comment on the effects of the irony and sarcasm used. Here are some things you could mention:
	•	The use of sarcasm to insult Brendan, indicating the writer's dissatisfaction with his service e.g. "highly skilled telephone operative".
	•	The writer's use of irony to express how much he dislikes the call centre process. He describes spending "twenty thrilling minutes" listening to hold music — his ironic tone shows his frustration at how long he had to wait.
	•	The use of irony in phrases like "slight hitch" and "lofty ambition" to add some humour to the text, which emphasises how ridiculous the writer finds the company.
5.	All your points should use relevant examples and terminology, and comment on the effects of the irony and sarcasm used. Here are some things you could mention:
	•	The use of sarcasm in Hafsa's exchange with her father, ("we'll have a great time"), which suggests she's quite cheeky or disrespectful.

Answers

Answers

- The use of irony in Kirsty's narrative, "It really was going to be a fun-filled night", "it seemed like the fun never stopped". This conveys her strong dislike of schoolwork.
- The use of sarcasm when insulting Miss Hayward ("Very on trend.") to indicate that both girls can be cruel.

Pages 36-37: Rhetoric and Bias

1. a) hyperbole   b) parenthesis   c) antithesis
2. E.g. "Who has not felt outraged at the injustice of the world when viewing images of child poverty?"
   Technique: Rhetorical question
   Effect: It makes the reader believe that "outraged" is the only reasonable reaction to have.
3. Evidence might include:
   - gives the writer's opinion as fact ("By far the best hobby")
   - makes generalisations, e.g. it claims that all young people "adore" playing cribbage
4. All your points should use relevant examples and terminology, and comment on the effects of the rhetorical devices used. Here are some things you could mention:
   - Use of rhetorical questions such as "have you ever dreamt of... escaping on a luxury break?" to make the reader think about doing exactly that.
   - Repeated use of lists of three, e.g. "lions, zebra and gazelle", to persuade the reader that there are many exciting options available to them.
   - The use of hyperbole to present a persuasive impression of the luxury nature of the holidays, such as "satisfy your every desire" and "your every wish will be catered for".
5. Answers should clearly compare the different ideas and techniques in each text, using quotations to support points. Here are some things you could mention:
   - The 19th-century writer has a fairly balanced viewpoint: they acknowledge positive aspects, like the room's size, as well as negative aspects, such as the "limited refreshment". This makes the writer seem more reasonable.
   - The writer of the 21st-century review has a more negative viewpoint than the writer of the 19th-century letter — they instantly "doubted" that the bedding was clean, which, combined with a complete absence of positive points about the room, shows that the writer is quite biased.

Page 38: Descriptive Language

1. Answers should pick out two examples of each technique from the text. Examples might include:
   Descriptive verbs: "burning", "trudged", "shimmered"
   Imagery: "cutting lines like knives", "I felt as if I were underwater"
2. ii) Evidence might include:
   - The use of a simile to make the noise easy to imagine.
   - The onomatopoeic description of the "buzzing" stadium, which helps the reader to imagine the excitement.
3. Your answer should offer an opinion on the statement. It should comment on the techniques used to describe the party, using relevant examples and terminology to support each point. Here are some things you could mention:
   - The cumulative effect of using several descriptive verbs together in "joking, laughing, making introductions", to convey a sense of action and excitement to the reader.
   - Onomatopoeic verbs such as "thumping" and "clinking" to help the reader to imagine what the party sounds like.
   - The focus on describing colours in the second paragraph, which appeals to the senses to help the reader to visualise the upbeat mood of the party.

Page 39: Narrative Viewpoint

1. a) first-person   b) third-person   c) second-person

2. Answers need to give an example from the text and explain why it's effective in the first person. E.g. The first-person narrator is effective in this extract because it allows an insight into the character's private emotions: the reader knows that she is feeling "terror" despite the fact that she has a "smile" on her face.
3. All your points should use relevant examples and terminology, and comment on the effects of the narrative viewpoint used. Here are some things you could mention:
   - The third person allows an insight into all of the characters' lives, which helps the reader to get to know their personalities. E.g. we know that the "young man" is nervous about his job interview, as well as about the "exhaustion" of the "middle-aged woman".
   - The third person creates tension, because it can comment on the things that the characters aren't aware of: "a murder has been committed". This dramatic irony makes the reader care about the characters, as they have a sense of what's in store for them.

Pages 40-41: Structure — Fiction and Non-Fiction

1. a) iii)   b) i)   c) ii)
2. a) description   b) setting   c) outside, inside
3. E.g. The paragraphs separate each individual piece of advice, which makes it easier for the reader to take in and remember the information.
4. All your points should use relevant examples and terminology, and comment on the effects of the structural features used. Here are some things you could mention:
   - The shift in time that the extract uses — it starts in the present day, goes back to the past, then returns to the present. This allows the reader to become emotionally invested in Joan, so the ending has a greater impact.
   - The progression from "she had already been looking forward to the next visit", to "there wouldn't be a next visit", which creates interest by emphasising the sadness of the fact that Joan's life is drawing to a close.
   - The motif of Joan looking at the sea, which is revisited in the first and last paragraph, and is contrasted by the way she "raced into the sea" in the second paragraph. This structure adds interest by making the ending of the story more poignant.
5. All your points should use relevant examples and terminology, and comment on the effects of the structural features used. Here are some things you could mention:
   - The repeated references to the writer's "Granny", which persuade the reader by continually linking baking to family love and the "unhurried life of a retiree".
   - The use of paragraphs to separate the writer's individual points in the second and third paragraphs, making it easier for the reader to follow the writer's argument.
   - The inclusion of a counter-argument in the fourth and fifth paragraphs, which allows the writer to acknowledge and dispel any doubts the reader may have about baking.

Pages 42-43: Sentence Forms

1. a) complex   d) complex
   b) compound   e) complex
   c) simple   f) compound
2. b) command. E.g. Commands create an authoritative tone, so a writer might use one to convince readers to take action.
   c) question. E.g. Questions make the reader think about their own response, so a writer might use one in order to get the reader on their side.
   d) exclamation. E.g. Exclamations are used to convey strong emotions, so a writer might choose this to help to persuade readers that they are passionate about what they're saying.

Answers

3. All your points should use relevant examples and terminology, and comment on the effects of the sentence forms used. Here are some things you could mention:
   - The long, complex sentence in paragraph one, which helps to build the reader's anticipation regarding the show.
   - The three consecutive short questions at the end of the second paragraph, which act as a cliffhanger to create a sense of Mikhail's panic and worry.
   - Sentences becoming generally shorter towards the end of the extract, to gradually increase the tension.

4. All your points should use relevant examples and terminology, and comment on the effects of the sentence forms used. Here are some things you could mention:
   - The use of a short sentence to begin the extract, which is dramatic and draws the reader in.
   - The very short exclamations "Faster!" and "Still faster!" to increase the pace of the extract when Jane is about to win the race, which creates interest for the reader.
   - The long, complex sentence that begins "Thousands and thousands of people", which suggests that the response to Jane's triumph is overwhelming.

Pages 44-45: Presentation

1. E.g. The numbered list makes the order of the different stages of the process clear.

2. a) Feature: headline
   Effect: e.g. uses alliteration to draw the reader's attention to the sensational nature of the story.
   b) Feature: picture
   Effect: e.g. shows the reader how peaceful and idyllic the village is, which makes the crime seem more shocking.
   c) Feature: subheading
   Effect: e.g. summarises the paragraph that follows and highlights the importance of the "appeal" to the reader.

3. All your points should use relevant examples and terminology, and comment on the effects of the presentational devices used. Here are some things you could mention:
   - The use of a short, sharp headline ("SAVE OUR CYCLISTS") to make the writer's argument seem urgent.
   - The use of the alliterative subheading "Dangerous and deadly" to grab the reader's attention and make them want to read the paragraph that follows.
   - The second subheading ("Time to change") emphatically states the writer's opinion, creating an authoritative tone that encourages the reader to agree with their viewpoint.
   - The use of a picture to grab the reader's attention and emphasise the large number of cyclists who use the roads.

4. All your points should use relevant examples and terminology, and comment on the effects of the presentational devices used. Here are some things you could mention:
   - The short, factual title is used to instantly tell the reader what the article will be about in a clear, informative way.
   - The subheading "An Island Paradise" persuades the reader to visit by suggesting that the island is somewhere special.
   - The photographs make the island seem beautiful, so the reader is given a further incentive to want to visit it. They also illustrate some of the written information, making the article seem truthful and accurate.

Section Four — Writing: Creative and Non-Fiction

Pages 46-47: Writing with Purpose

1.

Informative writing	Persuasive writing
an impersonal tone technical terms	rhetorical questions emotive language

2. Answers should include three separate points and a conclusion that summarises the argument, e.g.
   1) Gives a sense of identity within the school community.
   2) Means everyone looks the same, so they won't be bullied about their fashion choices.
   3) Counter-argument: Uniform is expensive. However, works out cheaper — don't have to buy fashionable clothes.
   Conclusion: School uniform is cheaper, and makes for a more equal school community.

3. E.g. Hiding away in the sleepy village of Lyttlewich, Howtonshire, is a true gem of English architecture that you can't afford to miss. Thousands of visitors flock to the ancient Lyttlewich Church every year to marvel at its truly stunning artwork. Isn't it about time you joined the crowd?

4. Answers need to reflect form, purpose and audience using suitable vocabulary and language techniques. Writing needs to be well-organised, clear and technically accurate. Here are some techniques you could include:
   - Rhetorical questions: "Do you really care about TV more than your health and wellbeing?"
   - Lists of three: "The more sleep you get, the happier, healthier and brainier you'll be."
   - Emotive language: "It's absolutely vital that you get enough sleep: your health and happiness depend on it."

5. Answers need to reflect form, purpose and audience using suitable vocabulary and language techniques. Writing needs to be well-organised, clear and technically accurate. Here are some techniques you could include:
   - Facts and statistics: "Studies show that students involved in the arts are twice as likely to do well later in life."
   - Repetition: "The arts help students to grow emotionally. The arts help students to communicate better. And above all, the arts help students to express their feelings."
   - Clear point of view: "Creative subjects such as Art and Drama are important and enriching areas of study."

6. Answers need to be entertaining for a general, adult audience. They need to use interesting language techniques to create a suitable tone and style. Writing needs to be well-organised, clear and technically accurate. These answers are for option (a), 'The Bike Race'. Here are some techniques you could include:
   - A dramatic opening: "Dwight's heart hammered as he pushed frantically against the pedals."
   - Varied sentence structures: "Wham! The cyclist slammed into him, sending them both careering across the track."
   - Descriptive words and phrases: "Dwight thrust his feet at the unforgiving ground, his pedals spiralling swiftly."

Pages 48-49: Writing for an Audience

1. b) E.g. The ear bones are some of the smallest in the body.
   c) E.g. Roman soldiers used throwing weapons to defeat their enemies.

2. a) E.g. Money can be tricky to get your head around, so why aren't schools teaching us how to deal with it?
   b) E.g. Your health is important — and eating well is the single easiest thing you can do to maintain a healthy lifestyle.

3. E.g. I wish to complain about the quality of the fruit in the supermarkets of Townton. It is simply impossible to locate an unbruised apple, no matter how attentively one searches.

4. Answers need to be entertaining for a general, adult audience. They need to use interesting language techniques to create a suitable tone and style. Writing needs to be well-organised, clear and technically accurate. These answers are for option (a), 'The Boat Trip'. Here are some techniques you could include:
   - An interesting opening: "They were going to crash."
   - Metaphor: "The waterfall was thunder; nothing else could be heard over its deafening roar."

Answers

- A cliffhanger ending: "They were safe for now, but there was a darker danger lurking just over the horizon."

5. Answers need to reflect form, purpose and audience using suitable vocabulary and language techniques. Writing needs to be well-organised, clear and technically accurate. Here are some techniques you could include:
   - Alliteration: "Don't risk roaming the roads — stay safe on the pavement."
   - A short sentence: "You face this danger every day."
   - A memorable closing line: "Awareness of road safety can save lives — perhaps one day it will save yours."

6. Answers need to reflect form, purpose and audience using suitable vocabulary and language techniques. Writing needs to be well-organised, clear and technically accurate. Here are some techniques you could include:
   - Facts and statistics: "The city plays host to over a million tourists every summer."
   - Antithesis: "This small town packs a big punch when it comes to restaurants, bars and eateries."
   - Hyperbole: "It's quite simply the best city in the world."

Pages 50-51: Creative Writing

1. engage; middle; character; direct; attention; clichés
2. a) E.g. First person, to give an insight into the character's thoughts and feelings.
   b) E.g. "Eerie", to make the forest seem scary and sinister. "Timid", to make the character seem afraid.
   c) E.g. "The moon was shining as brightly as a new penny."
3. a) E.g. I took a deep breath and stepped onto the alien spaceship, ready for my next adventure.
   b) E.g. The familiar sounds of the river rushing outside my window were all I needed to hear; I was finally home.
4. Answers need to be entertaining for a general, adult audience. They need to use interesting language techniques to create a suitable tone and style. Writing needs to be well-organised, clear and technically accurate. These answers are for option (c), 'Write about your local area.' Here are some techniques you could include:
   - A list of adjectives: "The fields were endless, fragrant and golden in the sun's light."
   - An unusual character: "The town's oldest resident, Agatha Hart, was a tiny lady who wore layers of colourful clothing that made her look at least twice her diminutive size."
   - Direct address: "Perhaps you might think that nothing exciting could ever happen in a sleepy town like Drizzleford. You'd be wrong."
5. Answers need to be entertaining for a general, adult audience. They need to use interesting language techniques to create a suitable tone and style. Writing needs to be well-organised, clear and technically accurate. These answers are for option (a), 'The Penguin.' Here are some techniques you could include:
   - The five senses: "The smell of fish was overwhelming. Jurgen fought down the urge to gag as he inhaled the aromas of the penguin enclosure."
   - Onomatopoeia: "The penguin's wings slapped excitedly."
   - A neat, satisfying ending: "The time had come; Jurgen returned the baby penguin to its mother, smiling wistfully at his memories of the fun they'd had."
6. Answers need to be entertaining for a general, adult audience. They need to use interesting language techniques to create a suitable tone and style. Writing needs to be well-organised, clear and technically accurate. These answers are for option (c), 'Write about a train journey.' Here are some techniques you could include:
   - An intriguing opening: "The train that carried Steve out of the city was exactly the same as the one he'd arrived on, after that fateful day all those years ago."

- Descriptive verbs: "The train slogged and toiled its way along the tracks."
- Personification: "The houses of the city seemed to watch him reproachfully as the train sped away."

Pages 52-53: More Creative Writing

1. E.g. The gnarled branches of the towering tree soared in the wind, scattering leaves all over the sparse grass underneath.
2. a) E.g. The old car was as rusty as an abandoned railway track.
   b) E.g. The street lights were tree trunks in the jungle of the city.
   c) E.g. My face flushed as red as a tomato with shame.
3. Answers should include ideas for the plot and characters of a story involving a castle. For example:
   1) Girl lost in woods — sees 'abandoned' castle — goes inside
   2) Hears voices — two men talking about committing a crime
   3) Tries to run / ring police — accidentally makes a noise
   4) Criminals chase — eventually escapes them
4. Answers need to be entertaining for a general, adult audience. They need to use interesting language techniques to create a suitable tone and style. Writing needs to be well-organised, clear and technically accurate. These answers are for option (c), 'Write about an interesting building.' Here are some techniques you could include:
   - Metaphor: "The seats are an ocean of blue fabric."
   - The five senses: "You can hear your footsteps echo as you walk over the wooden boards."
   - Onomatopoeia: "The curtains swish across the stage."
5. Answers need to be entertaining for a general, adult audience. They need to use interesting language techniques to create a suitable tone and style. Writing needs to be well-organised, clear and technically accurate. These answers are for option (a), 'Reaching New Heights.' Here are some techniques you could include:
   - The five senses: "The sun felt warm on Heather's face."
   - Metaphor: "The mountain was a formidable enemy, and Heather had conquered it."
   - Descriptive language: "The crisp mountain air whipped painfully at the climbers' exposed skin."
6. Answers need to be entertaining for a general, adult audience. They need to use interesting language techniques to create a suitable tone and style. Writing needs to be well-organised, clear and technically accurate. These answers are for option (b), 'Going Camping.' Here are some techniques you could include:
   - The five senses: "The air smelt of damp vegetation."
   - Personification: "The leaves whispered in the night."
   - A first-person narrator: "I shivered with cold as a brisk winter breeze crept into our tent."

Pages 54-55: Writing Articles

1. a) Purpose: to argue. Audience: pupils and teachers.
   b) E.g. Is our school not an ethnically diverse community?
   c) E.g. 38% of Wingwood's students are practising Christians.
2. E.g. There are those who argue that we don't do enough to protect endangered species, but I see evidence of the human race's efforts everywhere I look.
3. b) E.g. Unlucky for you, kids — according to the government, it's officially 'no adult, no access' to public places.
   c) E.g. We've had a real scorcher of a weekend, as temperatures rocketed sky-high in a totally unexpected heat wave.
4. Answers need to reflect form, purpose and audience using suitable vocabulary and language techniques. Writing needs to be well-organised, clear and technically accurate. Here are some techniques you could include:
   - Hyperbole: "Classical music is humanity's greatest accomplishment; its loss would be incomprehensible."
   - Rhetorical questions: "How have we let it go this far? Other industries have adapted, why not us too?"

Answers

- Lists of three: "How any listener can fail to be moved by Schubert's symphonies, Mahler's marches or Mozart's melodies is beyond me."

5. Answers need to reflect form, purpose and audience using suitable vocabulary and language techniques. Writing needs to be well-organised, clear and technically accurate. Here are some techniques you could include:
   - Direct address: "You shouldn't spend too long staring at the screen of your tablet or smartphone."
   - Imperative verbs: "Get into the habit of doing something active at least twice a week."
   - Reassuring language: "It's okay if you haven't tried a sport before — most sports clubs welcome beginners."

6. Answers need to reflect form, purpose and audience using suitable vocabulary and language techniques. Writing needs to be well-organised, clear and technically accurate. Here are some techniques you could include:
   - Conversational style: "I'd take a boat trip over travelling by aeroplane any day of the week."
   - Rhetorical questions: "Would you really rather cram yourself into an uncomfortable, overcrowded aeroplane?"
   - Lists of three: "Boats are better for the environment, for your health, and for your stress levels."

Pages 56-57: Writing Leaflets and Travel Writing

1. place; magazines; opinions; entertain; conversational; first
2. a) Leaflet
   b) E.g. It uses layout features such as bullet points.
3. E.g. THE CHIPS ARE DOWN FOR FAST FOOD
   Do you care about the survival of the independent restaurants in our local area? If so, then you'll surely agree that it's time we banned fast-food chains for good.
4. Answers need to reflect form, purpose and audience using suitable vocabulary and language techniques. Writing needs to be well-organised, clear and technically accurate. Here are some techniques you could include:
   - Direct address: "On Oakfall Island, there are dozens of different activities for you and your family to try."
   - Rhetorical questions: "Stuck for something to do this summer? Sick of visiting the same old places?"
   - Superlative adjectives: "It's simply the best holiday you'll ever have."
5. Answers need to reflect form, purpose and audience using suitable vocabulary and language techniques. Writing needs to be well-organised, clear and technically accurate. Here are some techniques you could include:
   - A clear heading: "GCSEs — How To Decide".
   - Imperative verbs: "Talk to teachers or older students to work out which subjects are right for you."
   - A friendly tone: "Making these decisions can feel tough at times, but there will be help and support available to you."
6. Answers need to reflect form, purpose and audience using suitable vocabulary and language techniques. Writing needs to be well-organised, clear and technically accurate. Here are some techniques you could include:
   - Descriptive adjectives: "We should leap at the chance to swap humdrum, drizzly British life for something new."
   - First-person narrative: "In Bermuda, I saw a sunset so beautiful that it brought tears to my eyes."
   - Analogy: "Trying to understand different cultures without going out and experiencing them is a little like trying to paint a portrait of something without ever seeing it: basically, you're bound to get it wrong."

Pages 58-59: Writing Reports, Essays and Reviews

1. a) Report   b) Review
2. a) E.g. Whilst there are conflicting opinions on the issue, it seems clear on balance that we must scrap the tuition fee.

b) E.g. The idea is completely inadvisable.
c) E.g. My conclusion is that the council should invest its funds into a new community centre.

3. Answers should include an introduction, three clear points and a conclusion that summarises the argument, e.g.
   Introduction: Outlines main argument.
   1) Space programmes require lots of funding, which would be better spent on hospitals and schools.
   2) Counter-argument: we can't live on Earth forever. But if we scrap space programmes, we can also invest in green energy so that we can live here longer.
   3) People have died exploring space (give examples).
   Conclusion: We should scrap most space exploration in order to invest in other, more important things.
4. Answers need to reflect form, purpose and audience using suitable vocabulary and language techniques. Writing needs to be well-organised, clear and technically accurate. Here are some techniques you could include:
   - Clear, objective language: "The glottalbug is not an endangered species."
   - Facts and statistics: "Around 75% of our local agriculture relies on the glottalbug."
   - Linking phrases: "On the other hand, the glottalbug has caused significant environmental damage in other parts of the country."
5. Answers need to reflect form, purpose and audience using suitable vocabulary and language techniques. Writing needs to be well-organised, clear and technically accurate. Here are some techniques you could include:
   - Counter-arguments: "Some argue that lowering the wages of footballers will result in an exodus of talent from the UK, but evidence from other countries suggests otherwise."
   - Facts and statistics: "The average wage of a top-flight footballer in the United Kingdom is almost 62 times that of the working population as a whole."
   - Balanced tone: "Whilst some footballers do donate to charity, it does not appear to be a widespread practice."
6. Answers need to reflect form, purpose and audience using suitable vocabulary and language techniques. Writing needs to be well-organised, clear and technically accurate. Here are some techniques you could include:
   - First-person narrative: "I utterly adored this film."
   - Hyperbole: "This film is a true giant in its genre; in thousands of years' time, we will still be talking about it."
   - Analogy: "This film does for the romance genre what John Wayne did for the Western."

Page 60: Writing Speeches

1. a) F   b) T   c) T
2. b) E.g. What will we do when all the landfill sites are full?
   c) E.g. We must take better care of our planet!
   d) E.g. The landfill sites are heaving with decomposing food, unwanted packaging and broken appliances.
3. Answers need to reflect form, purpose and audience using suitable vocabulary and language techniques. Writing needs to be well-organised, clear and technically accurate. Here are some techniques you could include:
   - Direct address: "Fellow restaurant-owners, I'm appealing to you to make a decisive move."
   - Repetition: "And whilst pizza is high in fat, high in calories and high in carbohydrates, it's also delicious."
   - Rhetorical questions: "We all love pizza, don't we?"

Page 61: Writing Letters

1.

Purpose	to argue
Audience	local council members
Register	formal

Answers

2. a) End: Yours sincerely
   b) Start: E.g. Dear Maria, End: E.g. Best wishes
   c) Start: Dear Sir / Madam, End: Yours faithfully
3. E.g. "If year 11 students aren't provided with somewhere they can relax and study in peace, their stress levels will grow and their studying will become more difficult. Both of these things could result in a dip in grades across the board."
4. Answers need to reflect form, purpose and audience using suitable vocabulary and language techniques. Writing needs to be well-organised, clear and technically accurate. Here are some techniques you could include:
   * Formal language: "Dear sir, I write to express my concern over the proposal to build more houses in rural areas."
   * Anecdotal evidence: "I have witnessed my local area destroyed by an influx of new, poor quality housing."
   * Linking phrases: "Moreover, rural building projects often pose a real danger to local wildlife."

Section Five — Sample Exams

Page 65: Paper 1, Question A1 — Sample Answer

1. 3 marks out of 5
   E.g. Answers 1, 2 and 5 are all correct and can be found in lines 1-8. Answer 3 would not get a mark as it does not say it is raining. Answer 4 would not get a mark as the streams aren't mentioned in this part of the text.

Page 67: Paper 1, Question A2 — Sample Answers

2. 5 marks out of 5
   E.g. This answer makes some insightful comments about language and structure as well as their effects and their influence on the reader. Technical terms are used accurately and examples are used effectively to back up points.

Page 69: Paper 1, Question A3 — Sample Answers

1. 5 marks out of 10
   E.g. The answer mentions the impression given of the shepherd and some of the animals, and it begins to comment on the effect of language. It could analyse the effect of the language and the influence on the reader in more detail though. It has used some relevant examples to back up the points, but it needs to use more technical terminology.
2. 8 marks out of 10
   E.g. This answer makes several accurate points covering the sheep, the dog and the shepherd, each backed up with good examples. The answer explores the influence on the reader in the second paragraph, but could go into more detail with this in the first paragraph. It could also go into more detail when analysing the effect of language.

Page 71: Paper 1, Question A4 — Sample Answers

1. 10 marks out of 10
   E.g. This answer makes detailed and insightful comments about the effect of both language and structural features, and how they influence the reader. Sophisticated subject terminology is used accurately, and there are well-chosen examples to back up the points.
2. 3 marks out of 10
   E.g. This answer makes some simple comments about the text, but doesn't clearly explain how it is made vivid or interesting. Some attempt has been made to use examples from the text, but there is no clear explanation of their effect on the reader.

Page 73: Paper 1, Question A5 — Sample Answers

1. 4 marks out of 10
   E.g. Some personal opinions on the statement have been given, and there has been an attempt to write about how the writer has created effects, backed up with some examples. The effects aren't explained in much detail though, and there isn't much use of technical terminology.
2. 7 marks out of 10
   E.g. This answer offers critical opinions on the statement, and starts to discuss how successful the whole text is (in the second paragraph). There is some analysis of how the writer has created effects. It could go into more detail in explaining effects and evaluating the statement.

Page 75: Paper 1, Section B — Sample Answers

1. Communication and organisation = 11 marks out of 24
   Vocabulary, sentence structure, spelling and punctuation = 10 marks out of 16
   Total = 21 marks out of 40
   E.g. The communication and organisation could do with some improvement — it attempts to use some structural features and language devices, but they're not always effective (e.g. "lit his face like a torch"), so the text isn't very engaging for its audience. There's one spelling mistake and the answer could vary its punctuation and sentence forms more.
2. Communication and organisation = 23 marks out of 24
   Vocabulary, sentence structure, spelling and punctuation = 12 marks out of 16
   Total = 35 marks out of 40
   E.g. The communication and organisation is imaginative and engaging — there is an interesting structure that starts by describing the scene then narrows down to the child and his thoughts. The answer uses a good range of vocabulary and sentence structures, and it controls the present tense well, but the punctuation could be more varied, and there is one punctuation error ("oak Street").

Page 80: Paper 2, Question A1 — Sample Answer

1. 2 marks out of 3
   E.g. The answers to parts (a) and (c) are correct. The answer to part (b) is incorrect — she says that the letter is only to be read by Branwell (her brother), not her father or aunt.

Page 81: Paper 2, Question A2 — Sample Answers

2. 9 marks out of 10
   E.g. Appropriate quotations are used to illustrate interesting points, with technical terms used accurately throughout. Some points are expressed unclearly (e.g. "appeal to the relationship between"), so the answer doesn't get full marks.

Page 82: Paper 2, Question A3 — Sample Answer

1. 2 marks out of 3
   E.g. For part (a), "Children" is correct but "their nannies" is incorrect. The two groups Albelli is referring to are children and their parents. The answer to part (b) is correct.

Page 83: Paper 2, Question A4 — Sample Answers

1. 3 marks out of 10
   E.g. This answer has given some simple personal opinions on the text and has identified some of the writer's views. The points are not always backed up with evidence from the text though, and there is very little explanation of how the writer has created effects.
2. 6 marks out of 10
   E.g. The answer shows understanding of the writer's views, and begins to evaluate how the writer has created effects. Examples are used, but they could be better explained.

Answers

Page 85: Paper 2, Question A5 — Sample Answers

1. 2 marks out of 4
   E.g. This answer selects a range of relevant details from both texts, and shows a basic understanding of why the relationship between parents and a nanny can be difficult. It doesn't combine the details to create an overview though.
2. 4 marks out of 4
   E.g. This answer makes concise points that show a clear understanding of why the relationship between parents and a nanny can be difficult. It combines details from both texts to give an overview, and points are supported by relevant examples.

Page 87: Paper 2, Question A6 — Sample Answers

1. 10 marks out of 10
   E.g. The answer makes interesting, detailed points about the writers' points of view, comparing them confidently and fully explaining the methods that each writer uses. It also supports each point with useful, precise evidence.
2. 4 marks out of 10
   E.g. Some similarities and differences between the attitudes of the two writers are identified, supported by some relevant quotes. However, the quotes aren't analysed to explain the writers' methods, and some quotes, such as "riotous", are used inaccurately. The comparisons aren't always explained clearly, especially in the final sentence.

Page 89: Paper 2, Questions B1 and B2 — Sample Answers

1. Communication and organisation = 9 marks out of 12
   Vocabulary, sentence structure, spelling and punctuation = 7 marks out of 8
   Total = 16 marks out of 20
   E.g. The answer is written clearly and is well suited to its form, purpose and audience. It could be improved by more consistently adapting its register to the audience, for example by cutting out colloquial expressions such as "In a nutshell". The answer is accurately written, with a good range of vocabulary, but to get full marks it could include a more interesting range of punctuation and sentence forms.
2. Communication and organisation = 4 marks out of 12
   Vocabulary, sentence structure, spelling and punctuation = 3 marks out of 8
   Total = 7 marks out of 20
   E.g. There has been some attempt to match the writing to the form, purpose and audience required, but it is inconsistent. The language is also too informal — so the register is not appropriate for the audience. There has been some attempt at structure. Spelling is occasionally inaccurate, and there needs to be more variety of punctuation, vocabulary and sentence structures.

Section Six — Practice Exams

Pages 90-91: Paper 1

A1. 1 mark for each valid response given, up to a maximum of five marks. Answers might include:
   - He lives in a small town.
   - He is eight years old.
   - He usually goes to bed at nine or nine-thirty.
   - He sometimes asks his parents if he can stay up later to listen to the radio.
   - He lives in a small house.
   - He lives on a small street.
   - He wants some ice cream.

A2. All your points should use relevant examples and terminology, and comment on the effects of the language used. Here are some things you could mention:
   - The writer's choice of the verbs "run" and "thump" show that the child is hurrying on his trip. This helps to convey the child's eagerness for the ice cream to the reader. His haste is further emphasised through the contrast with the slowness of Mrs Singer, who moves "ponderously".
   - The writer describes sounds to make the description vivid to the reader. Onomatopoeic verbs such as "slap" and "thump" stand out to the reader when presented against the "quiet and far off" town. This focuses the reader's attention on a few, clear details, which helps them to vividly imagine the child's trip.

A3. All your points should use relevant examples and terminology, and comment on the effects of the language and structure used and its influence on the reader. Here are some things you could mention:
   - The writer presents the child's mother as kind. The fact that she "smiles" despite being "hot and irritated" demonstrates that she does not take any of her irritation out on her child. This kind impression is furthered by her fairness in thinking of others: she divides the ice cream up, leaving some for the father and brother who aren't present. The cumulative effect of these actions is to make the reader like and sympathise with the child's mother.
   - The writer describes Skipper, the child's older brother, in detail using a long list of adjectives: "healthy, red-faced, hawk-nosed, tawny-haired, broad-shouldered". In this way the reader is shown that he is strong and energetic. The long list would also leave the reader breathless if spoken out loud, which reinforces this impression of Skipper's lively character.

A4. All your points should use relevant examples and terminology, and comment on the effects of the language and structure used and their influence on the reader. Here are some things you could mention:
   - The description of the child eating the ice cream has a calming effect on the reader. The image of the child at the "core" of the "deep quiet summer night" helps you to imagine how profoundly quiet it is, and the child is simply "enjoying" his ice cream in the middle of it, which shows how content he is. This might remind the reader of a moment of calm in their own life.
   - Sentence forms are used to create a sense of the monotony in the child's life. The list of the records he has listened to is long; the word "and" is also repeated, which has the effect of lengthening the sentence further, suggesting the child has played the records many times. When combined with the word "exhaustion", the effect is to demonstrate that he is so tired of them that he is prepared to simply sit and stare out the door instead.

A5. Your answer should evaluate the text by giving an opinion on the statement. It should comment on the techniques the writer has used to make the passage tense, using relevant examples and terminology to support each point. Here are some things you could mention:
   - The writer successfully makes the passage tense by contrasting the mood of the child (Doug) with his mother's mood. In lines 45-46 the mother's doubt is shown by her feeling that Skipper "should be home", whereas Doug is confident: he knows "very well" that Skipper will come home. This contrast creates tension as the reader knows something is wrong, whilst Doug does not, so the reader is left waiting for Doug's innocent belief to be broken.

Answers

- Tension is also created through the use of imagery. He feels a "coldness" that he can't explain: this representation of his building anxiety helps the reader to imagine how he is feeling, so that they begin to feel tense too.

B.   Answers need to be entertaining for a general, adult audience. They need to use interesting language techniques to create a suitable tone and style. Writing needs to be well-organised, clear and technically accurate. These answers are for option (b), 'The Misty Morning.' Here are some techniques you could include:
   - An interesting, dramatic opening sentence: "The mist appeared too suddenly for them to avoid it."
   - Direct address: "If you'd seen what I saw on that misty October morning, you'd have done the same thing."
   - Similes: "Just past the end of the jetty, waiting like a promise, was the little red boat."
   - Contrasting descriptions: "A brisk, fresh winter breeze began to blow, rapidly clearing the clammy tendrils of stagnant fog."

Pages 93-94: Paper 2

A1.   a) They first met at university.
     b) She rang at 6pm.
     c) They might be 70.

A2.   All your points should use relevant examples and terminology, and comment on the effects of the language and structure used and their influence on the reader. Here are some things you could mention:
   - Jenni Russell has structured her article to support her assertion that friends are important. At the start, she uses an example to demonstrate the negative effects that friends can have: Jo's loss of her "confidante" was "one of the worst things" she'd ever experienced. Russell then finishes the article with the suggestion that friendship is worth it: people "live longer and are happier" with close friends. This structure allows her to show the reader that she understands the complexities of friendship, so they would be more likely to trust her view that friends are important.
   - The writer uses language to relate to the reader and create a friendly, inclusive tone. In the penultimate paragraph, she repeats the pronoun "we". The effect of this is to make the reader feel as if the writer shares and understands the problems that readers have, so they would be more likely to listen to and trust her.

A3.   a) Because he doesn't have any friends.
     b) Because he's afraid that he will see someone who wants to borrow money from him during the daytime.
     c) Susan.

A4.   Your answer should evaluate the text by giving an opinion on it. It should comment on the techniques the writer has used to convey his views on his Boisterous Friend, using relevant examples and terminology to support each point. Here are some things you could mention:
   - Wilkie Collins shows that he finds his Boisterous Friend annoying by using animal imagery to describe his behaviour: his laugh is described as a "roar" and he "rushes in like a mad bull". These descriptions help the reader to sympathise with Collins's viewpoint, as they make his friend's behaviour seem out of control.
   - The reader may feel that Collins is being overly harsh on his friend. They have known each other since they were children and the Boisterous Friend loves him "like a brother", yet Collins says that he could "dispense" with him. This could make the reader feel that Collins is being ungenerous to his friend.

- However, he does not ultimately "dispense" with his friends, as is shown by him allowing his friend in at the end. As such, it seems likely that his annoyance with his Boisterous Friend is at least partly affectionate. Readers may therefore find his views amusing as they may relate them to similar friends that they have.

A5.   Answers should use relevant quotes or examples from both texts to clearly answer the question. Here are some things you could mention:
   - Both writers show that relationships with other people can interfere with your own plans. Russell's friend Jo had planned to go to the cinema, but her plan was disrupted by Genevieve cancelling on her. Collins is planning to go home to finish writing an article, but thinks that he may not have "a clear five minutes" to do so because of interruptions from his friends.
   - Wilkie Collins shows that relationships can be problematic because people may try to use you. For example, he writes about his friend who borrows money from him and how he is an "obvious nuisance".
   - Russell shows that it "isn't easy" to maintain friendships and that losing a friend can be emotionally distressing. Her friend Jo's experience of losing a friend was "one of the worst things" that had ever happened to her.

A6.   Answers should clearly compare the different attitudes and techniques in each text, using quotations to support points. Here are some things you could mention:
   - Collins seems to find friendship tiresome: the way he lists the friends he could "dispense" with in the penultimate paragraph emphasises his desire to part with them. Russell, in contrast, believes that there are "powerful reasons" for maintaining friendships. The word "bonds" suggests that she feels friendships are strong ties that should not be broken.
   - Collins is writing satirically. His terms of familiarity, such as "dear", hint at a true fondness for his friends, and his complaint that one friend "never does" ask him to dinner could imply that he does want to socialise, which suggests that he has a positive attitude towards friendship after all. Russell, in contrast, writes with an earnest tone to offer a genuine answer to her title question: "What are friends for?" Readers might be amused by Collins's article, whilst Russell is aiming to share her thoughts and potentially inspire readers to work hard at their friendships.

B1.   Answers need to reflect form, purpose and audience using suitable vocabulary and language techniques. Writing needs to be well-organised, clear and technically accurate. Here are some techniques you could include:
   - Formal vocabulary: "It is often perceived that new students suffer most from a lack of confidence."
   - Facts and figures: "For 7 out of 10 new students the main difficulty was a lack of openness from existing pupils."
   - Clear, direct language: "Firstly, we must educate existing students in the need to be welcoming to newcomers."
   - A serious tone: "The importance of this transition period cannot be underestimated."

B2.   Answers need to reflect form, purpose and audience using suitable vocabulary and language techniques. Writing needs to be well-organised, clear and technically accurate. Here are some techniques you could include:
   - Conversational style: "I think the writers of this proposal need to take a good, long look at themselves."
   - Rhetorical techniques: "Who on Earth actually believes that this can be achieved?"
   - Direct address: "I invite you (and all readers) to carefully consider your opinion on this proposal."
   - A list of three: "This proposal is old-fashioned, restrictive and deeply unpopular."